Letts



SUCCESS FOR SCHOOLS

GCSE SHORT COURSE

# CITIZENSHIP

Kim Richardson

# CONTENTS

## UNIT 1 RIGHTS AND RESPONSIBILITIES


Citizenship . . . . . 4
Rights and responsibilities in action . . . . . 6
Human rights . . . . . 8
Changing society . . . . . 10


## UNIT 2 MAKING AND APPLYING THE LAW


How laws are made . . . . . 12
The English legal system . . . . . 14
Crime and the criminal courts . . . . . 16
Keeping the peace . . . . . 18
Changing society . . . . . 20


## UNIT 3 THE DEMOCRATIC SYSTEM


What is democracy? . . . . . 22
A short history of democracy . . . . . 24
How Britain is governed . . . . . 26
Elections and political parties . . . . . 28
Regional and local government . . . . . 30
Changing society . . . . . 32


## UNIT 4 COUNTRIES AND IDENTITIES


What is the UK? . . . . . 34
Where do we come from? . . . . . 36
Multicultural Britain . . . . . 38
Prejudice and discrimination . . . . . 40
Changing society . . . . . 42


## UNIT 5 THE MEDIA


What is the media? . . . . . 44
Controlling the media . . . . . 46
Representing society . . . . . 48
Bias in the media . . . . . 50
Changing society . . . . . 52

## UNIT 6 BRITAIN'S ECONOMY

The economic system ........ 54
Types of business ........ 56
Running the economy ........ 58
Changing society ........ 60

## UNIT 7 WORKING AND SPENDING

A working life ........ 62
Equal opportunities at work ........ 64
Consumers' rights ........ 66
Changing society ........ 68

## UNIT 8 THE UK, EUROPE AND THE WORLD

The growth of the EU ........ 70
Spotlight on the EU ........ 72
Citizens of Europe ........ 74
Flashpoint Europe ........ 76
The UK and the world ........ 78
Changing society ........ 80

## UNIT 9 ONE WORLD

Globalisation ........ 82
Rich world, poor world ........ 84
Trade and aid ........ 86
The global environment ........ 88
Changing society ........ 90

Glossary ........ 92

# CITIZENSHIP

**What does it mean to be a citizen?**
**Any definition of citizenship must focus on two important ideas – rights and responsibilities.**

## RIGHTS

Citizens have certain rights and freedoms which allow individuals to live, act and fulfil their potential free from interference from other individuals or from the state.

There are three kinds of rights associated with citizenship:

- **civil rights** – the citizen's rights in law, such as freedom of speech, freedom of belief, the right to own property and the right to a fair trial
- **political rights** – the right to take part in political processes, such as the right to vote and the right to stand for office
- **social rights** – the right to a certain standard of living, such as income support, state-funded education and public health.

These rights are laid down in various conventions of human rights pp.8–9 and upheld by the rule of law p.12.

## RESPONSIBILITIES

Citizens also have certain responsibilities. Without some sense of duty or obligation to each other and the community, society would break down.

There are three kinds of responsibility:

- **social and moral responsibility** – showing respect and responsible behaviour to those around you and to those in authority
- **responsibility to the community** – being aware of and involved in the life and concerns of your neighbourhood (school, community, town, etc.)
- **political responsibility** – being aware of and involved in the institutions and practices of democracy, at local, regional and national levels.

Many of these responsibilities are fulfilled voluntarily by citizens, such as voting or care for the environment.

Other responsibilities are imposed on citizens through the rule of law, both civil law (e.g. outlining the duties of employees) and criminal law (e.g. prohibiting violence to the person).

## WHICH COMMUNITY?

A narrow, legal definition of citizenship applies the term to that group of people who are formally recognised by the state. British citizenship, by this definition, depends on various factors, such as whether you were born in the UK and whether your parents are British citizens.

Many people argue for a wider definition of citizenship in which the state is not so central. They point to several factors which undermine the importance of the state:

- Our strongest links are often with our local communities, not the state.
- Decentralisation of power from Westminster has given more power to the regions p.30.
- The Human Rights Act 1998 applies to all individuals in the UK, not just people who are legally citizens p.9.
- Globalisation demands that we have responsibilities and rights within a global context, e.g. in the areas of pollution and poverty pp.82-83.

It may be more useful to view citizenship as a spectrum, in which rights and responsibilities are recognised at many different levels.

rights

INDIVIDUAL — FAMILY — LOCAL — REGIONAL — NATIONAL — EUROPEAN — GLOBAL

responsibilities

# BALANCING RIGHTS AND RESPONSIBILITIES

People have different views about what the balance in society should be between rights and responsibilities.

I believe that **responsibilities** are more important than rights. Citizenship should emphasise the social role of the citizen far more than the individual's rights. Rights on their own lead to selfishness and irresponsibility. Shared goals and the life of the community are more important than individual self-interest.

I believe that **rights** are more important than responsibilities. The state is a necessary evil, which restricts my ability to act as I wish. The emphasis in citizenship should be on protecting my individual rights. This will allow me to act independently and pursue my own interests. The only responsibility I have to the community is to protect these rights, and the rights of others.

I believe that **rights and responsibilities** shouldn't be in opposition to each other, but are dependent on each other. We are all individuals, but we are also rooted in the community. Through participation in the community we both protect our rights and promote social justice.

**Active citizenship recognises that:**
**(a) our rights depend on the recognition of others' rights**
**(b) rights and responsibilities come together in the political process: citizenship is a two-way process.**

**Key Words**

active citizenship • citizenship
decentralisation • globalisation
responsibility • right

## ACTIVITIES

1. **Work with a partner to try and define citizenship in one sentence in your own words.**
2. **Read the three different views above on the balance of rights and responsibilities in society. Which view do you agree with, and why?**
3. **Answer questions on Worksheet 1.**

# RIGHTS AND RESPONSIBILITIES IN ACTION

**We have rights and responsibilities in every area of society. Other units in this book discuss what our rights and responsibilities are at work** pp.62–65**, as a consumer** pp.66–67**, as a voter** pp.22–23 **and as a member of a multicultural society** pp.38–43**. Here we look at rights and responsibilities closer to home – in the family and at school.**

## IN THE FAMILY

### PARENTAL RESPONSIBILITY

Parents have the responsibility to care for the physical, moral and emotional needs of their children until they are 18. This parental responsibility is designed to benefit the child, not the parent.

Parental responsibility is not spelled out clearly and in detail in any single law in England and Wales, but it is generally understood to cover the following areas of family life:

- **Basic care**: the duty to feed and clothe their children properly, and to ensure they get the right medical treatment.
- **Education**: the duty to see that their children have suitable full-time education, and the right to choose the school.
- **Discipline**: the right and duty to discipline their children, although physical punishment must be 'moderate and reasonable'.
- **Religion**: the right to decide in which religion to bring up their children.

Parents who are married share parental responsibility for their children. If the parents are unmarried, only the mother has automatic parental responsibility – the father must apply for it.

### Marriage ...

- You have the right to marry at 16, although you need your parents' or guardians' consent if you are under 18.
- Married couples have the legal duty to look after each other and support each other financially. Unmarried couples do not have this duty.
- Married couples have equal rights to occupy their home. If couples are not married, the non-owner of the home only has this right if the couple draw up a contract in law.

### ... and divorce

- If married couples separate, the marriage is still valid in law.
- If couples wish to end their marriage by divorce, they must prove to a court that the marriage has 'irretrievably broken down'.
- If divorcing parents cannot agree on where their children will live, they may eventually need to go to a court. The court will decide in the best interests of the child, and will take the child's own views into account.

After a divorce, both parents keep parental responsibility for their children.

# AT SCHOOL

## SOME RIGHTS

*Parents have the right:*

- *to choose the school for their child, though they may be refused their choice*
- *to educate their child out of school*
- *to withdraw their child from religious education and sex education lessons.*

*Pupils have the right:*

- *to free school meals if their parents are on a low income*
- *to see their school records.*

*Teachers have the right:*

- *to punish pupils, including detention after school if this is reasonable and parents are given notice*
- *to confiscate certain items, e.g. mobile phones, though they must return them at the end of the day.*

*Schools have the right:*

- *to insist that pupils wear uniform, if it is reasonable and does not discriminate on grounds of sex or race*
- *to exclude pupils as a last resort, though parents have the right to appeal against permanent exclusion.*

## SOME RESPONSIBILITIES

*Parents have the responsibility:*

- *to ensure their child is suitably educated between the ages of five and 16*
- *to make sure that their child receives full-time education, either at school or otherwise.*

*Pupils have the responsibility:*

- *to behave sensibly and reasonably at school*
- *to obey school rules.*

*Teachers take on some of the responsibility of parents when pupils are in their care (in loco parentis).*

*Schools have the responsibility:*

- *to ensure that their pupils are safe when in school, and to take steps to prevent bullying*
- *to provide pupils with religious education and sex education*
- *to send parents a written report on their child's/children's progress at least once a year.*

*The state has the duty to provide children with free education, though charges may be made for music tuition, trips, etc.*

## ACTIVITIES

1. Write down three rights and three responsibilities that parents have towards their children. Is there a good balance between rights and responsibilities?
2. Marriage is a legal contract. What are the advantages and disadvantages of this?
3. Investigate the different rights and responsibilities that pupils in different years have in your school. (For example, do they have to wear uniform? What duties do they have?) Are the differences justified in each case?
4. Answer questions on Worksheet 2 about parental responsibility in question 1; the rights of 16-year-olds in question 2; the nuclear family in question 3; and giving advice in question 4.

# HUMAN RIGHTS

**There is an international dimension to rights, called human rights. What are human rights, where have they come from, and how are they applied?**

## A SHORT HISTORY OF HUMAN RIGHTS

People in the West have made many attempts to establish basic rights to protect their life and liberty. Some of the most important milestones in this struggle are shown below.

**1215 Magna Carta (Britain)**
Issued by King John, this established important rights and principles for 'all free men', e.g. the right to be consulted about taxes and the right to a fair trial. It became the basis for the concept of natural justice.

**1689 Bill of Rights (Britain)**
This set out certain rights and freedoms that English subjects could claim against the King (William III), e.g. that he was not allowed to suspend the laws, as James II had done.

**1776 Declaration of Independence (USA)**
This is the foundation document of the USA, which declares that all people are 'created equal' and have 'inalienable rights' to 'life, liberty and the pursuit of happiness'.

**1789 Declaration of the Rights of Man and the Citizen (France)**
This stated the new principles that lay behind the French Revolution: that 'men are born free and remain free and equal in rights' p. 24.

**1948 Universal Declaration of Human Rights (United Nations)**
This was designed to protect the rights of everyone in the world after the abuses of the Second World War. It begins: 'All human beings are born free and equal in dignity and rights'. In 30 'articles' it defines some fundamental rights, e.g. those of 'life, liberty and security of the person', 'freedom of movement' and 'freedom of thought, conscience and religion'. The Declaration forms the basis of the UN Commission on Human Rights p. 79.

**1959 Declaration of the Rights of the Child (United Nations)**
This sets out some basic rights for children, e.g. the rights to equality, love, health and a decent standard of living, play and protection from cruelty. It forms the basis of the UN Convention on the Rights of the Child.

**1963 European Convention on Human Rights (Europe)**
This was passed to support human rights throughout Europe. It is based on the UN Declaration of Human Rights, but excludes certain rights, such as those to housing, work and education. It is upheld by the European Commission on to Human Rights, which may pass cases on to the European Court of Human Rights in Strasbourg.

**1998 Human Rights Act (Britain)**
Although the European Convention on Human Rights has supported human rights in Europe for nearly 40 years, the procedure for pursuing justice has been complex, costly and time-consuming. If British citizens felt that their rights were violated, they had to take their case through the whole system of UK courts before having it heard in the European Court of Human Rights in Strasbourg. In 1998, therefore, the UK government made the European Convention on Human Rights part of UK law.

# WHAT ARE HUMAN RIGHTS?

**Human rights are the rights to which all humans are entitled.**

**The rights are set out in conventions (or codes), and countries that sign up to the conventions are then bound by international law. This means that they agree to uphold the rights in their countries, although the codes do not automatically become part of the law of each country.**

## FIVE KEY POINTS ABOUT THE HUMAN RIGHTS ACT

1. The Act is a major historical milestone – it brings the UK into line with most other European states in defining fundamental rights and guaranteeing them in law.
2. This means that existing laws must be interpreted in the courts in a way that is compatible with the Convention.
3. Public bodies, such as the police, prisons and local councils, must also act in a way compatible with the Convention.
4. The Act protects basic freedoms, such as liberty, security, the right to a fair trial, and freedom of speech, thought and religion.
5. It also limits these rights if other people's freedom is being infringed, or in unusual circumstances such as war or national emergency.

The Human Rights Act strikes a balance between the rights of the individual, their responsibilities and the interests of a democratic society.

Article 10 states, for example: 'Everyone has the right to freedom of expression'.

The right to freedom of expression is a basic democratic right, which allows individuals, such as journalists, to express controversial or disturbing views.

However, the right may be limited to protect national security and the reputations of others, or to prevent incitement to religious or racial violence.

## ACTIVITIES

1. In pairs, look at the historical milestones on page 8. What similarities are there between the rights proclaimed at each 'milestone'? Why do you think they are so similar?
2. Look at the UN Declaration on the Rights of the Child on Worksheet 3 and answer the questions there.
3. Search for the details of the Human Rights Act 1998 on www.hmso.gov.uk

   Explain (a) why the Human Rights Act 1998 is important, and (b) how it manages to balance the rights and responsibilities of individuals.

# CHANGING SOCIETY

**Your rights may appear to have been handed down to you by the state or the international community. This is a passive view of citizenship rights, which tends to make us feel powerless and helpless to make any changes ourselves.**
**An active approach to citizenship recognises that rights are won through campaigns and struggle. Individuals and groups do have the power to change society for the better. This power is part of becoming more responsible citizens.**

## WORKING FOR HUMAN RIGHTS IN THE UK: LIBERTY

Individuals usually look to specialist pressure groups to support them in their causes p. 32. One such group is Liberty, an independent organisation that works to defend rights and freedoms in England and Wales. Founded in 1934, it is the largest membership organisation of its kind in Europe.

The main ways in which Liberty works are:

- to lobby parliament
- to pursue human rights test cases through the courts
- to challenge human rights abuses and get the law changed
- to provide human rights advice to individuals and groups
- to work with the media to keep human rights issues in the public eye.

Along with other groups, Liberty campaigned for over ten years to get the government to incorporate the European Convention on Human Rights into UK law. This eventually happened in 1998 with the Human Rights Act pp. 8–9.

www.liberty-human-rights.org.uk 

## APPLYING THE HUMAN RIGHTS ACT 1998

The Human Rights Act only came into force in the UK in October 2000, so it is still unclear exactly how it will affect people's everyday lives. However, there are countless areas where individuals could invoke the Act if they feel their rights have been abused. Here are just three examples:

- **A pupil is excluded from school** for three months for bad behaviour. Her parents feel the punishment is unfair and challenge the exclusion in court under Article 2 of Protocol 1 of the Act – 'No person should be denied the right to education'.
- **A member of the Romany community is refused planning permission** by the local council to keep a caravan on his land. The applicant challenges the decision in court under Article 8 of the Act – the 'right to respect for private and family life'.
- **A gay couple wish to marry**, but are forbidden under UK law. They challenge that law by invoking Article 12 of the Act – 'the right to marry and found a family'.

# WORKING FOR HUMAN RIGHTS IN THE WORLD: AMNESTY INTERNATIONAL

*Every year thousands of people across the world have their human rights abused. Although organisations such as the UN Commission on Human Rights try to monitor these abuses and liaise with governments to improve human rights, they need the help of campaigning organisations and pressure groups such as Amnesty International. Through its thousands of volunteers, Amnesty works to:*

- *free all political prisoners – those imprisoned because of their political, religious or other beliefs, or because of their race or social status*
- *ensure that political prisoners have a fair trial*
- *abolish torture and the death penalty.*

*Amnesty does this by investigating human rights abuses, lobbying governments and campaigning for the release of individual prisoners. Members of Amnesty write letters which:*

*1. target the government holding the prisoner*

*2. provide publicity to the media*

*3. keep up the morale of the prisoner.*

*Amnesty's success in supporting individuals and helping to change the law was recognised when it was awarded the Nobel Peace Prize in 1977 and the United Nations Human Rights Prize in 1978.*

www.amnesty.org.uk 

# BECOMING RESPONSIBLE PARENTS: PARENTLINE PLUS

Parenting is a vitally important but difficult job, and it involves huge responsibilities. Being a responsible parent is a significant part of being a responsible citizen.

Parentline Plus is one organisation that helps people to become more responsible parents. It does this by:

- running parenting courses where groups of parents get support on the issues they face
- working with children and adults during difficult times such as divorce and separation
- offering advice and information to families through its freephone helpline and website.

www.parentlineplus.org.uk 

## ACTIVITIES

**Key Words**

active citizenship • human rights
pressure group • responsibility
right

1. Write down four ways in which individuals or groups can improve our rights or responsibilities as citizens.
2. Look at the three imaginary test cases to the Human Rights Act on page 10. Should the Human Rights Act support the appeals of the excluded pupil, the Romany and the gay couple? Write a short paragraph on each case, giving reasons for your answers.
3. Discuss whether you think that there should be parenting classes at school.
4. Answer questions on Worksheet 4 on supporting and opposing protesters in question 1, and your reactions to corporal punishment in question 2.

## EUROPEAN LAW

- *European law applies in Britain because Britain is a member of the European Union (EU). Indeed, European law has supremacy over national law.*
- *The various bodies of the EU are responsible for making European law* p.72 ➤*. The process is complex to allow for a lot of consultation (see flowchart).*
- *EU laws take the form of regulations and directives. Regulations automatically become law in each member country. Directives require states to pass their own laws to bring the directive into effect.*

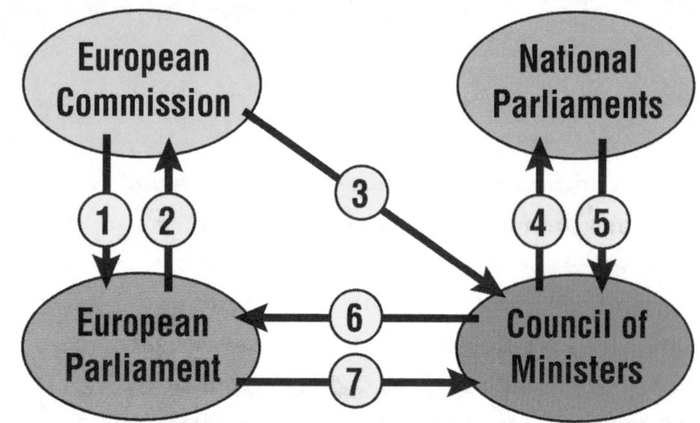


1 The Commission proposes an EU law to the European Parliament
2 The European Parliament discusses/amends it and passes it back
3 The Commission drafts a firm proposal and sends it to the Council of Ministers
4/5 The Council of Ministers discusses/amends it, consulting their national Parliaments
6 The Council sends its 'common position' on the proposal to the European Parliament
7 If the European Parliament approves, the Council adopts the new law; if the Parliament rejects, the Council can still adopt law if it is unanimous.

# HOW LAWS ARE MADE

- **In an ideal world, everyone would behave responsibly voluntarily. In the real world, however, we have to control behaviour by encouraging or rewarding people, or by threatening disapproval or punishment. These are informal kinds of social control.**
- **In many cases, compulsory rules of behaviour are required, which are recognised and applied by the state. These formal forms of social control are called laws.**
- **The system of laws and customs that sets out the powers of government and states the rights of citizens is called the constitution. The British constitution is based on the three main kinds of law: statute law, common law and European law.**

## COMMON LAW

- Many of our laws do not come from Acts of Parliament but from common law. These are the unwritten laws that have developed from centuries of custom and tradition.
- Common law is made by judges, who base their judgements on precedent – past decisions of the courts that act as a guide to the present. If the point of law in a case has not been decided before, whatever the judge decides forms a new precedent for future cases to follow.
- Most civil law and a lot of criminal law is common law. Murder, for example, is a common law crime as it has never been defined in an Act of Parliament.

Judges also have the power to interpret (define) statute law, to report on the actions of public bodies (judicial review) and to overrule aspects of laws that conflict with constitutional rules or human rights (constitutional review).

# STATUTE LAW

Laws passed by Parliament are called statutes or Acts of Parliament. About 60 Acts are passed each year. Most of these are introduced to Parliament by the Government as part of its overall policy, or legislative programme pp.26–27.

Laws are proposed by the government as Bills, and are discussed by the Cabinet in their draft form. Bills have to pass through several stages in both Houses of Parliament (the House of Commons and the House of Lords) before they become law – see the flowchart (below).

Individual MPs and peers can also propose laws, called private members' Bills. The time allowed to debate these is limited, so few private members' Bills become law.

www.explore.parliament.uk 

## From Bill to Act

|  |  |
|---|---|
| 1 First Reading | The Bill is printed and made available for MPs and others to read. There is no debate. |
| 2 Second Reading | About two weeks later, the Bill is debated in the House of Commons and a vote is taken. |
| 3 Committee Stage | The Bill is referred to a Committee of MPs who debate it in detail and propose amendments (changes). |
| 4 Report Stage | The Committee sends a report to the House of Commons listing the amendments. These are then debated. |
| 5 Third Reading | The Third Reading follows immediately. It is the final vote on the Bill in the House of Commons. |
| 6 House of Lords | The Bill now goes through the same five stages in the House of Lords. Any amendments it makes then have to be approved by the House of Commons. |
| 7 Royal Assent | The monarch gives approval to the Bill, after which it becomes an Act of Parliament. |

### Key Words

Act of Parliament • Bill • civil law common law • constitution criminal law • House of Commons House of Lords

## ACTIVITIES

1. **In groups, discuss why we need laws.**
2. **Sort the cards on Worksheet 5 into three groups depending on whether the terms refer to statute law, common law or European law. Complete the two further questions on the law in this worksheet.**
3. **Why does the process of passing an Act of Parliament go through so many stages? Working with a partner, describe in one sentence each the reason for each of the stages in the flowchart above.**
4. **How much power do each of the following bodies have in the process of law-making in England and Wales: (a) House of Commons (MPs), (b) House of Lords, (c) the monarch, (d) judges, (e) the European Union. Give each a rating of 1 to 5 (1 being least power). Be prepared to explain your rating in a class discussion.**
5. **Log on to www.explore.parliament.uk and investigate further how a government proposal becomes law.**

# THE ENGLISH LEGAL SYSTEM

**The law in England and Wales covers a huge variety of situations. (Scotland has its own law and legal system.) This lesson looks at the two major types of law – civil law and criminal law – before focusing on resolving disputes in civil law.**

| CIVIL LAW | | CRIMINAL LAW |
|---|---|---|
| Civil law states what your rights and duties are in your dealings with other people | DEFINITION | Criminal law deals with offences against society |
| Disputes over contracts, property rights, discrimination, trespass, family issues (marriage, divorce) | EXAMPLES | Murder, violence, misuse of drugs, driving offences, fraud |
| To uphold the rights of individuals and settle matters between them | PURPOSE | To maintain law and order and protect society |
| Claimant v. defendant | THE TWO SIDES | Prosecutor (usually the state through the police and Crown Prosecution Service) v. defendant |
| County court or High court | COURTS | Magistrates' court or crown court |
| Judge | WHO DECIDES | Magistrates (in magistrates' court) or judge and jury (in crown court) |
| Liable or not liable | DECISION MADE | Guilty or not guilty |
| Award of damages or injunction, etc. (demands to act in a certain way) | POWERS OF COURT | Fine, community sentence, imprisonment |

The division in the legal system between civil and criminal law results in different kinds of courts (see below). At the top of the pyramid, the courts combine and can pass judgement in both civil and criminal cases.

Appeal courts review disputed decisions of the lower courts.

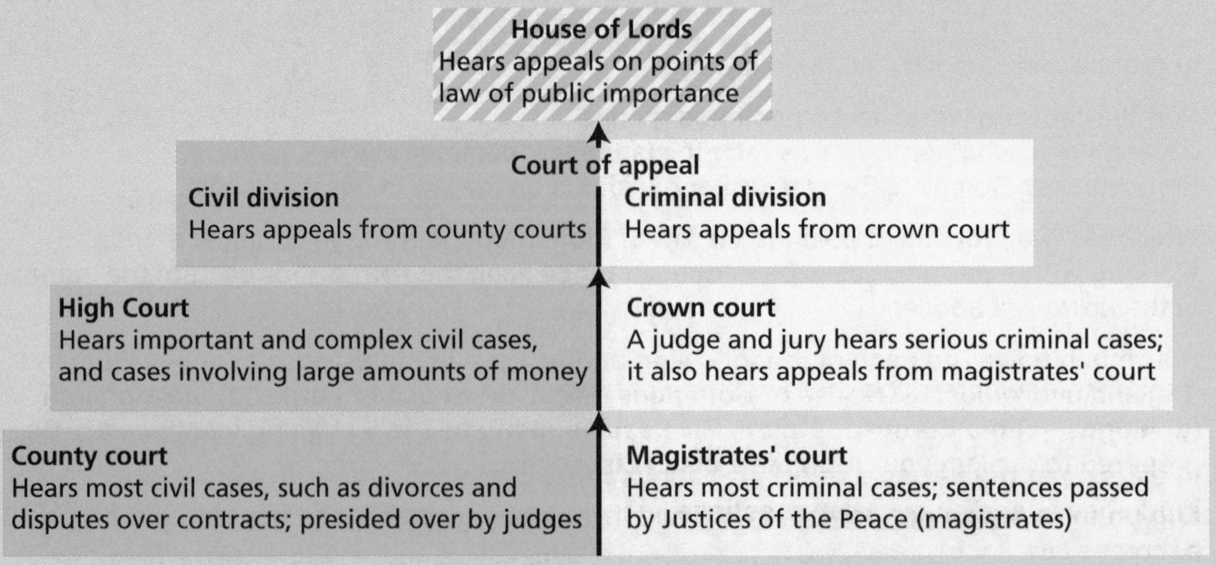

**House of Lords**
Hears appeals on points of law of public importance

**Court of appeal**

| Civil | Criminal |
|---|---|
| **Civil division** Hears appeals from county courts | **Criminal division** Hears appeals from crown court |
| **High Court** Hears important and complex civil cases, and cases involving large amounts of money | **Crown court** A judge and jury hears serious criminal cases; it also hears appeals from magistrates' court |
| **County court** Hears most civil cases, such as divorces and disputes over contracts; presided over by judges | **Magistrates' court** Hears most criminal cases; sentences passed by Justices of the Peace (magistrates) |

The court system in English law. The green boxes relate to civil law, the yellow boxes to criminal law.

## PEOPLE IN THE LAW

***There are two types of lawyer in England and Wales – solicitors and barristers. Together they make up the legal profession.***

**I'm a solicitor** at a high street firm. I advise my clients on a whole range of legal matters such as buying a house, business contracts or making a will. I negotiate on their behalf and do a lot of paperwork. Since 2000 I have been able to speak for them in all the law courts (advocacy). Other solicitors specialise in particular aspects of the law, or work for the Crown Prosecution Service or other public bodies.

**I'm a barrister**. Like most barristers, I'm self-employed. I mainly represent clients by speaking on their behalf in the courts (advocacy), but I also give advice and draft ocuments. Certain professions can come to me directly and brief me (instruct me to act for them), but clients usually have to go to a solicitor first, who then briefs me. I'm hoping eventually to become a judge.

## RESOLVING DISPUTES

Civil court cases are expensive, stressful and time-consuming, so most people try to resolve their disputes before they reach the court. There are several ways in which people can do this:

- **Direct negotiation** – explaining the problem, e.g. by taking a faulty item back to the shop, or writing a letter of complaint to the other side p.67 ➤.
- **Going to a solicitor** – who will then negotiate on the client's behalf and hope to settle 'out of court'.
- **Alternative Dispute Resolution** (ADR) – which includes mediation and conciliation (where a neutral mediator helps the two sides reach a compromise) and arbitration (where the two sides allow a third party to make a binding or unbreakable decision).
- **Tribunals** – such as social security, rent and employment tribunals, are composed of a panel of three adjudicators, who listen to the dispute and come to a resolution.

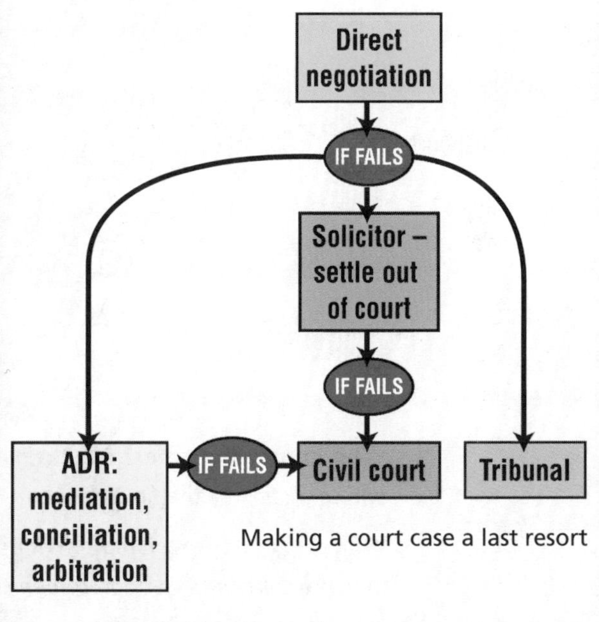


Making a court case a last resort

### ACTIVITIES

1. Explain in one paragraph the difference between criminal law and civil law.
2. In pairs, read the newspaper articles about court cases on Worksheet 6 and answer the questions.
3. Discuss the ways in which you could resolve a dispute without taking your case to court.

# CRIME AND THE CRIMINAL COURTS

**What is crime, how big a problem is it, and what happens to those who are arrested for committing an offence?**

## CRIME

*A criminal offence is an offence against the law of the land. As the pie chart shows, most crime is crime against property. Although violent crimes have been increasing recently, fewer than one in seven crimes involve violence, and a third of these are common assault where there is little or no injury.*

**Recorded crime, 2000/2001**

**(Source: The Home Office)**

Criminal damage 19%
960 087 offences

Theft and handling stolen goods 23%
1 176 925 offences

Fraud, forgery, drug and other offences 9%
496 019 offences

Violent crime 14%
733 326 offences

Theft of and from vehicles 19%
968 447 offences

Burglary 16%
836 027 offences

***Who commits crimes?*** *Most crime is committed by young men. A third of all men have at least one conviction by the time they are 40.*

***Who suffers crimes?*** *You are more likely to be a victim of crime if you live in an inner-city area than if you live in a rural area. Young men are most at risk of being attacked by a stranger; the elderly are least at risk.*

*Various causes of crime have been suggested:*

- *Low moral standards – some believe that people are not naturally law-abiding, and the influence of religion is declining.*
- *The increasing gap between rich and poor – the 'have nots' taking from the 'haves'.*
- *There are so many things to steal – especially valuable portable objects.*
- *A decline in the family unit – leading to a lack of emotional security.*
- *The thrill of law-breaking – especially for young men.*
- *The influence of drugs and alcohol – and the need to pay for the drugs habit.*

# THE LIFE HISTORY OF A CRIME

This diagram charts the history of a crime through the police and criminal courts system.

- *Over 95% of criminal cases are heard in magistrates' courts, presided over by unpaid magistrates, or justices of the peace (JPs). There is no jury.*
- When the accused is under 18, the case is usually heard in a youth court, a special kind of magistrates' court.
- Only serious cases are heard in the crown court, which is presided over by a judge. Juries consist of 12 adults chosen at random from the electoral register pp.20–21.

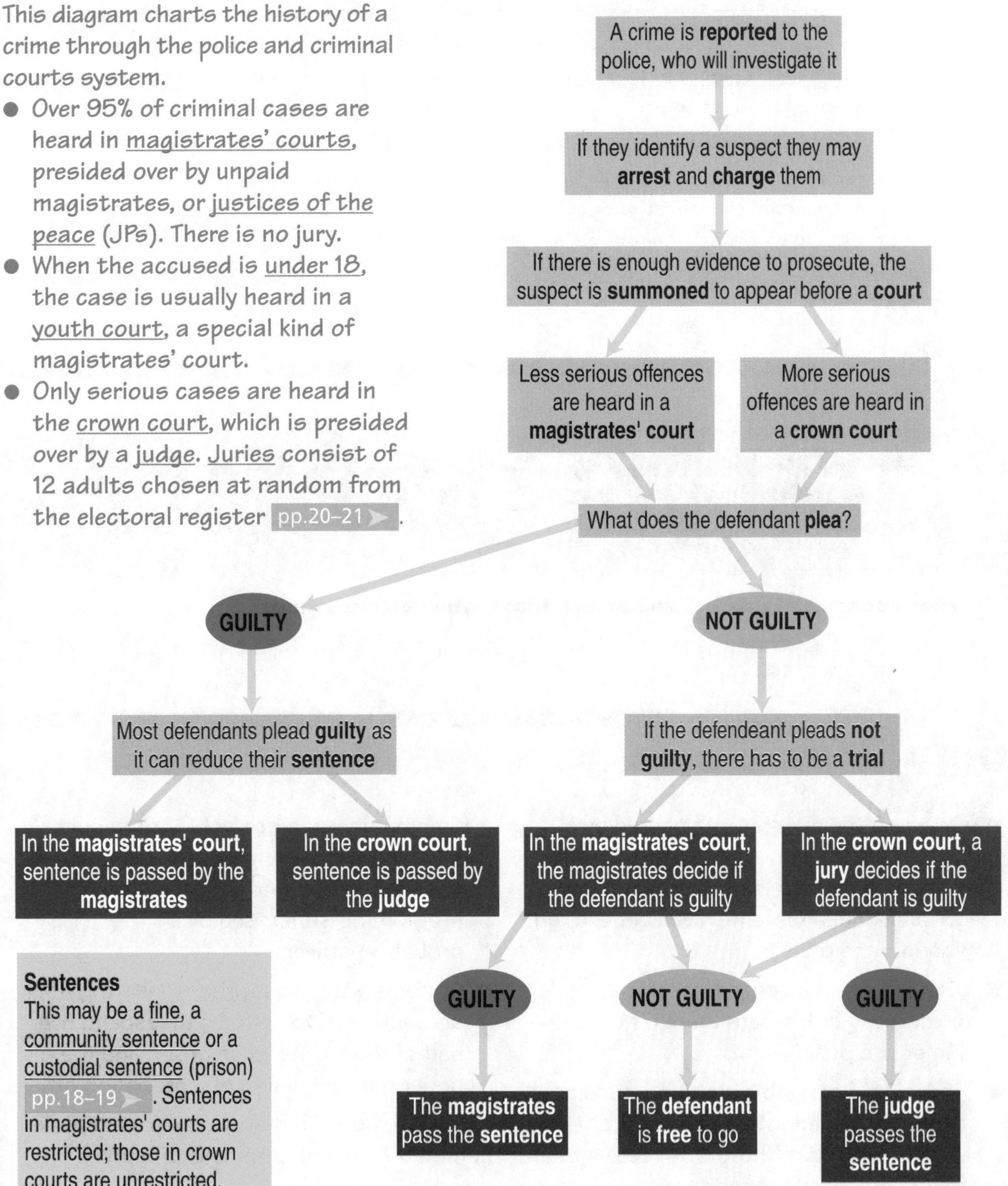

A crime is **reported** to the police, who will investigate it

If they identify a suspect they may **arrest** and **charge** them

If there is enough evidence to prosecute, the suspect is **summoned** to appear before a **court**

Less serious offences are heard in a **magistrates' court**

More serious offences are heard in a **crown court**

What does the defendant **plea**?

**GUILTY**

Most defendants plead **guilty** as it can reduce their **sentence**

In the **magistrates' court**, sentence is passed by the **magistrates**

In the **crown court**, sentence is passed by the **judge**

**NOT GUILTY**

If the defendeant pleads **not guilty**, there has to be a **trial**

In the **magistrates' court**, the magistrates decide if the defendant is guilty

In the **crown court**, a **jury** decides if the defendant is guilty

**GUILTY** — The **magistrates** pass the **sentence**

**NOT GUILTY** — The **defendant** is **free** to go

**GUILTY** — The **judge** passes the **sentence**

**Sentences**
This may be a fine, a community sentence or a custodial sentence (prison) pp.18–19. Sentences in magistrates' courts are restricted; those in crown courts are unrestricted.

**Key Words**
crown court • judge
jury • magistrates' court

## ACTIVITIES

1. **Write down three facts about magistrates' courts and three facts about crown courts.**
2. **Read again the reasons put forward for the causes of crime. In groups, discuss (a) which you think are the two top causes, (b) why you think so many young men get involved in crime.**
3. **Read the factsheet on jury service (Worksheet 7) and discuss the questions.**

## THE POLICE

- *The police have several duties: to protect people and property; to maintain public order; to prevent and detect crime; and to arrest criminals and bring them to court.*
- *The police have the power to stop you in the street and ask for your name and address. They can search you if they think you are carrying drugs, stolen goods, weapons or anything that might be used for theft or burglary.*
- *If a police officer arrests you, after questioning you can be charged with the offence or issued with a formal caution – a warning that if you commit further crimes you will be sent to court.*
- *The police supervise demonstrations and control large crowds at football matches, etc. If violence breaks out, they act to protect people and property.*
- *The police must obey the law and follow their own disciplinary code.*

# KEEPING THE PEACE

**How does society detect and punish those who commit crimes?**

## SENTENCING

A sentence is the punishment imposed by a judge or magistrate on an offender who has been found guilty in a criminal court. The length and kind of sentence given depends on how serious the crime is.

- Discharge – 9% of people receive a discharge, which means there is no immediate punishment.
- Fines – 71% of people are fined, a cheap sentence to administer and one as effective as other penalties (those who receive them are no more likely to reoffend).
- Community sentences – 11% of people have to do unpaid work in the community or attend other kinds of organised programme, supervised by a probation officer.
- Custodial sentences (prison) – 8% of people are sentenced to custody; they spend over half of their sentence in prison and the rest under the supervision of a probation officer.

The table shows the various theories that lie behind the idea of punishing offenders.

| Theory of punishment | Aim of punishment |
|---|---|
| 1 Retribution | To make the offender suffer for having committed a crime |
| 2 Deterrence | To discourage the offender (and others) from committing further crimes |
| 3 Protection | To protect society by locking up offenders |
| 4 Reform | To help the offender change their behaviour so that they will no longer commit crimes |

# PRISON

A custodial sentence is the most severe sentence that a court can give.

- In 2000 there was an average of 64 600 people in prison in England and Wales. Of these, 8070 were male young offenders (i.e. aged under 21), 3350 were women, and 10 570 were prisoners held on remand (i.e. awaiting trial or sentence). The remaining comprised 42 610 adult males.
- Most prisoners serve sentences of fewer than four years.
- Only a fifth of adult prisoners sentenced to immediate custody have committed violent crimes. The majority are in prison for sexual offences, drug offences, robbery, burglary and non-payment of fines.
- The prison population has increased steadily over the last 50 years, from 21780 in 1951 to 64 600 in 2000.

## DO PRISONS WORK?

Prisons often satisfy public demands for punishment and calm the feelings of victims, but critics believe that prisons should only be used as a last resort to protect society from violent criminals. The critics point to the following drawbacks of imprisonment:

- **Inefficiency**. Prisons don't appear to deter as most ex-prisoners return to a life of crime. 52% of all prisoners released in 1996 were back inside within two years, and rates are even higher for young offenders.
- **The 'university of crime'**. Prisons are where you can learn new crimes and make contact with other criminals. They can turn petty offenders into hardened criminals.
- **Cost**. It costs over £500 per week to keep someone in prison. To build a new prison costs the equivalent of two district hospitals.
- **Health**. The experience of being imprisoned can be too much for some offenders. In 2000 the Prison Service recorded 5175 incidents of self-harm, including 1500 attempted hangings.

## ALTERNATIVES TO PRISON

Prison reformers, such as the Howard League, suggest that two other approaches are more effective and humane than imprisoning offenders:

- **Non-custodial sentences**. All but the most serious offenders should be punished by fines, cautions or community sentences.
- **Crime prevention**. More money and effort should be put into preventing crime than into dealing with it once it has occurred.

### Key Words

community sentence
custodial sentence

## ACTIVITIES

1. In groups, discuss whether you think the police do a good job.
2. In pairs, look at the list of sentences that the courts can give offenders p.18. Discuss the aim of the punishment in each case. (There may be more than one.)
3. 'Imprisonment is the best way of taking criminals off the streets and protecting society.' Do you agree? Write two paragraphs giving your reasons. Quote evidence from these two pages in support of your views.
4. Log on to (a) www.payback.org.uk or (b) http://web.ukonline.co.uk/howard.league to investigate an organisation which campaigns to reduce the use of prison as a punishment.
5. Read the six case studies of offenders on Worksheet 8 and decide in groups what sentences you would give them. Answer the second question on this worksheet concerning the impact of life imprisonment.

# LAW REFORM

The law should adapt to the changing needs of society. Pressure to change the law can come from various quarters, such as the government, independent bodies and individual citizens.

## GOVERNMENT

The government published its plans to reform the criminal justice system in its white paper 'Justice for All' in 2002. In it the government proposes:

- allowing defendants who have been acquitted of very serious offences to be tried again on the same charge (the double jeopardy rule)
- speeding up the trial process and introducing greater consistency on sentences
- introducing several alternatives to prison sentences, e.g. a mixture of prison and community schemes
- allowing major fraud trials and other complex cases to be tried by a judge alone, without a jury.

## INDEPENDENT BODIES

Although the government has the greatest say in what laws should be passed, it has its own political agenda. An independent body – the Law Commission – was therefore set up in 1965 to 'keep the law under review'. The Commission:

- considers areas of law that are in need of reform
- suggests which laws are out of date and need to be repealed (abolished)
- suggests ways of simplifying and modernising the law.

More than two-thirds of the Law Commission's reports have become law. However, lack of debating time in Parliament, and the controversial nature of criminal law reform, has delayed much reform.

## INDIVIDUALS

Individuals, supported by a pressure group, can also show that the law needs changing. Here is one example.

*One woman, Mrs Day, felt it was unfair that she was not given any redundancy pay as she was a part-time worker. The Equal Opportunities Commission took her case to court in 1994. The House of Lords decided that the law was discriminating against women, which broke an important principle of European law. Parliament was forced to change the law and give employment protection rights to both full-time and part-time workers* pp.64–65.

# WORKING FOR JUSTICE

**There are several opportunities for people who are not legally qualified to be involved in the decision-making process of the courts. The most important of these are magistrates and juries.**

I am a magistrate, or Justice of the Peace. Along with 30 000 others in England and Wales, I'm effectively a part-time judge in the magistrates' courts. I get trained (some say not enough) but I don't get paid. Together, magistrates try over 95% of all criminal cases. My colleagues and I have often been criticised as 'middle-class, middle-aged and middle-minded', but I reckon I understand the problems of my local area pretty well.

I sell mobile phones in a high street store. I've just been called for jury service in a rape case in the crown court. There are 12 of us: together we have to decide whether the accused is guilty or not. We are given guidance by the judge, but the decision is up to us. I feel proud to be representing ordinary citizens in this democratic process, but I can't wait to get back to my shop.

# CHANGING SOCIETY

**The law and the courts can seem like a huge, complex and oppressive system over which we have no control. This lesson shows how the law and the legal system isn't set in stone, and that individuals and groups do have opportunities to change society in this area.**



## ACCESS TO THE LEGAL SYSTEM

*For all citizens to have equal access to the legal system, its cost and complexity need addressing. In recent years some attempts have been made to do this.*

### Cost

- *From 1998 barristers have no longer had a monopoly of representing clients in the courts. This should bring greater competition between solicitors and barristers and reduce costs.*
- *Poorer people who use the legal system have the costs of their cases refunded in full or in part. However, claims for personal injury are now excluded.*

### Efficiency and availability

*The introduction of the Community Legal Service (CLS) in 2000 was a major change to the system of legal assistance in England and Wales. CLS:*

- *co-ordinates in one network all legal and advice services, such as solicitors, advice agencies and local authorities, making people's access to the law greater and more efficient*
- *demands that all these organisations meet certain standards and display the CLS Quality Mark*
- *replaces the old system of legal aid with the CLS Fund, although it has also restricted its availability.*

*The aim is to have a CLS network in every area of England and Wales.*

### Modernisation

*The civil court service is investigating greater use of information technology to make access to justice faster, easier and cheaper. Its proposals in 2001 include:*

- *virtual courts – using the Internet, email and digital TV in straightforward cases such as small claims*
- *easier access – using telephone, Internet and email to provide information and access to the legal system, alongside the old methods of communicating in writing or attending in person.*

**Key Words**

civil law • criminal law • jury
magistrate • pressure group

## ACTIVITIES

1. What, in your opinion, made Mrs Day's case so important p.20?
2. Discuss the proposals to increase access to the legal system. Do you think there is equal access for everyone in society?
3. Would you want to (a) become a magistrate, (b) be called to jury service? In each case, write down three facts about what is involved, and three opinions about how important or effective a job it is.
4. The government has published controversial proposals to allow civilians to help police the streets as community support officers (CSOs). Read the article on Worksheet 9 and, in groups, discuss whether you agree with the idea of CSOs.

# WHAT IS DEMOCRACY?

**The word 'democracy' derives from the Greek word 'demokratia' and means 'people power' – rule by the people and for the people. Democracy works at national, local or grassroots level. Although there are other political systems in the world, democracy is the most common.**

## DEMOCRACY CHECKLIST

What are the important features of a government or organisation that make it democratic?

- **Rule by the majority.** The person or party with the most votes forms the government or leads the organisation. This government is authorised by the electorate to rule according to its programme. The final authority belongs with the people (popular sovereignty), as the power of the government is based on the will of the people.
- **Free and regular elections.** Elections must be free – that is, people must be allowed to express their opinions freely. Secret ballots are one feature that allow people to do this. Elections must also be regular and frequent to allow the people to exercise their choice and to dismiss governments they dislike.
- **Universal suffrage.** All adults must be allowed to vote and exercise other political rights, whatever their age, sex, wealth or race.
- **Rule of law.** Governments must act within the framework of agreed rules or laws p.12. A constitution usually defines how the government must behave and how laws are to be made. The UK and some other countries do not have a written constitution, but regard their laws and customs as defining the powers of the state.
- **Respect for individual rights.** One aspect of liberal democracies is that they respect the rights and freedoms of their citizens p.4.
- **Free flow of information.** There should be little or no censorship, and citizens should be properly informed p.46.

## FIVE CRITICISMS OF DEMOCRACY

Democratic systems have also been criticised, for several reasons:

1. **'You can't trust politicians'.** Some people believe that politicians are an elite political class more interested in their own advancement – or even abusing power – than in serving the public.
2. **'Governments are elective dictatorships'.** Others say that once every few years we vote for governments to do what they like until the next election pp.28–29.
3. **'Money talks'.** Some believe that behind the façade of democracy, the richest groups in society still take all the important decisions in their own interests.
4. **'What's it all about?'** It is thought that ordinary people don't always understand the complex issues facing modern society.
5. **'It's a media circus'.** Some people suggest that the political process is dominated by the media, which distorts and disguises the real issues pp. 46–51.

## OTHER POLITICAL SYSTEMS

Although nearly two-thirds of the world's nations are now democracies, many are not, including:

- totalitarian regimes, such as Cuba and North Korea. These are one-party systems that tightly control most aspects of public life and intrude into private life.
- authoritarian regimes, such as China and Iraq. These are one-party states and military dictatorships which violate human rights to a significant extent.
- traditional monarchies, such as Morocco and Saudi Arabia. In these states, most power is kept in the hands of the royal family, passed down from generation to generation.

# TYPES OF DEMOCRACY

There are many different ways in which governments and organisations can be democratic.

***Direct or representative democracy?***

- Direct democracy means that the people make the decisions and laws directly, at meetings attended by every citizen or member.
- Larger organisations, such as nation states, practise representative democracy: those who make the laws are chosen (elected) by the people to represent them.

***Weak or strong democracy?***

- Weak democracy distrusts the ability of ordinary people to govern themselves; a political elite runs the affairs of state.
- Strong democracy encourages direct participation in the political process, using pressure groups, direct action and referenda, etc.

***Unitary or federal states?***

- Unitary states, such as Britain, place full authority in their central government, which can overrule other institutions.
- Federal states, such as Germany, give limited powers to the central (federal) government; most powers are devolved to the individual provinces or states.

***Presidential or parliamentary systems?***

- In presidential systems of government such as the USA, the chief executive (president) is elected separately from the legislature or law-makers (Congress), who can therefore hold him or her to account.
- In parliamentary systems, such as Britain, the chief executive (prime minister) is the leader of the majority party of the legislature (MPs), so there is no separation of powers.

## ACTIVITIES

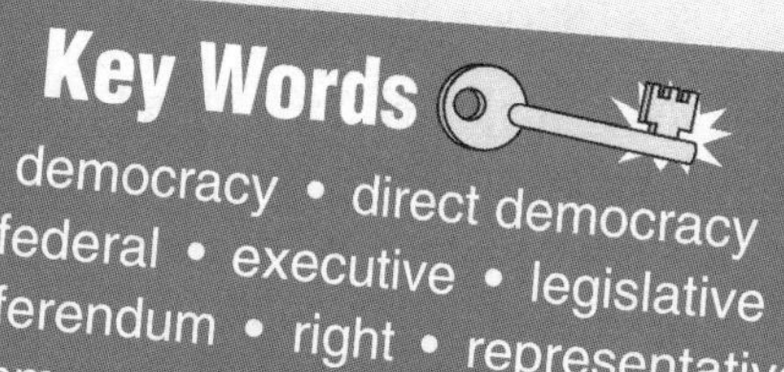


1. **In pairs, discuss the six features of democracy ('Democracy checklist', page 22). Which do you think is the most important feature? Explain your view in a class discussion.**
2. **In groups, discuss how democratic (a) your school, or (b) your home is. Use the democracy checklist to help you.**
3. **Log on to www.schoolcouncils.org and investigate how to set up either (a) a school council, or (b) a class council.**
4. **Read the case study on Worksheet 10. Work in groups to prepare your part of the case. Then answer the questions that follow.**
5. **Using the information in the table below, design cut-out cards and place in order under the two headings 'Strong democracy' at one end and 'Weak democracy' at the other. Be prepared to justify your choices in a class discussion.**

| Strong democracy | |
|---|---|
| **Weak democracy** | |
| Attending union meetings | Listening to the news on the radio |
| Voting in a general election | Standing for election as a local councillor |
| The government telling people what they should do | Complaining in the pub about the state of the nation |
| Joining a demonstration or protest march | Not voting because it is a waste of time |
| Complaining to your MP | Taking part in the school council |

# A SHORT HISTORY OF DEMOCRACY

**Democracy has evolved in different ways and at different rates across the world over two and a half thousand years.**

**c.450 BC** Direct democracy in Athens, Greece. The people's assembly meets about 40 times a year, and all adult male citizens have the right to speak and vote.

**c.200 BC** Highpoint of the republic in Rome, Italy. Two consuls are elected yearly as heads of state. The senate is dominated by the aristocracy and the wealthy; the people's assembly has less power.

**212 AD** Citizenship is given to every freeborn subject in the Roman empire.

**c.930** The Althing is established in Iceland – an assembly meeting each summer to pass laws and decide legal disputes. The Althing is the oldest surviving parliament in Europe.

**c.1100** Feudal societies in the Middle Ages are based on a hierarchy of power, with the monarch at the top and those who work the land at the bottom. Common people have no political rights, but rulers generally act within the law.

**1215** King John signs the *Magna Carta*, which limits the monarch's power and recognises the rights and liberties of his subjects p.8.

**1295** The Model Parliament, the first representative English parliament, is summoned by Edward I: two knights from each county, two burgesses (free men) from each borough and two citizens from each city.

**c.1450** Johann Gutenberg invents the printing press.

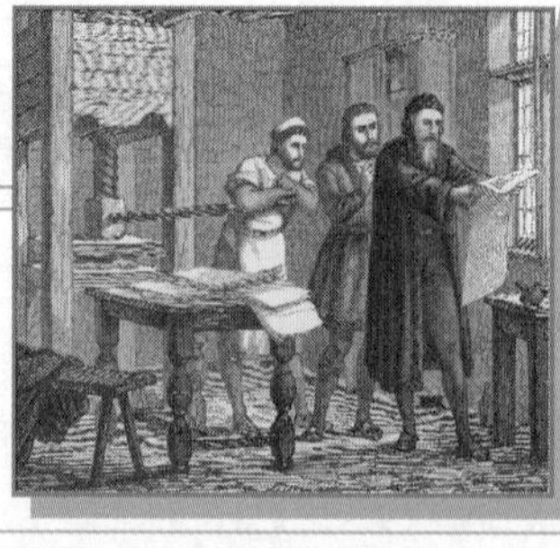

**c.1530** Acts of Parliament begin to replace royal proclamations as the source of new laws p.13.

**c.1600** Age of Absolutism in Europe: monarchs become more powerful than ever, and representative bodies are powerless or non-existent.

**1649** Charles I is executed after a civil war between Parliament and King. The monarchy and the House of Lords is abolished. A republic (Commonwealth) is proclaimed, but monarchy is restored in 1660.

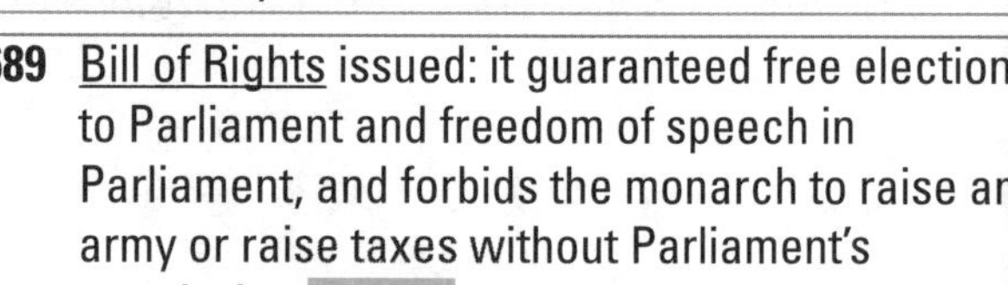

**1689** Bill of Rights issued: it guaranteed free election[s] to Parliament and freedom of speech in Parliament, and forbids the monarch to raise a[n] army or raise taxes without Parliament's permission p.8.

**1707** Union of England and Scotland: the first Parliament of Great Britain meets.

**c.1725** Sir Robert Walpole leads the government and chairs a small group of ministers on the King's behalf – the forerunner of the cabinet. He is no[w] regarded as Britain's first prime minister, thoug[h] he never accepted that title.

**c.1750** Height of the Enlightenment in Europe, an intellectual movement which criticised existing ideas and institutions: Montesquieu argues for the separation of powers p.23, and Rousseau writes *The Social Contract*, with its slogan 'Liberty, Equality, Fraternity'.

**1776** United States declares independence from Britain. The American colonists objected to paying taxes to Britain when they weren't represented in Parliament. The Declaration of Independence emphasises the importance of individual rights and liberty p.8. A federal government is later established, with George Washington as first president.

**1789** Start of the French Revolution: the people turn against the absolute monarchy. They declare a republic and execute King Louis XVI. A radical constitution gives the vote to all adult males, bu[t] war in Europe eventually leads to Napoleon becoming emperor p.8.

**c.1800** The Industrial Revolution creates a prosperous middle class and an industrialised working class based in the cities; this leads to demands to extend the franchise (the vote).

**1801** The Union of Britain and Ireland creates the United Kingdom pp.34–35 ➤.

**1832** The Reform Act extends the vote in the UK to the less wealthy middle classes. About a fifth of English adult males can now vote.

**1865** The defeat of the South in the American Civil War leads to the end of slavery there.

**1867** The Second Reform Act nearly doubles the electorate by extending the vote to the wealthier working classes.

**1872** The secret ballot is introduced for parliamentary elections. It becomes a permanent measure in 1918.

**1884** The Third Reform Act gives the vote to agricultural labourers.

**c.1900** Democracy spreads through the British Empire, leading to effective independence for Australia, Canada, New Zealand and South Africa. Native peoples still do not have the vote, however.

**c.1910** Suffragettes in Britain campaign for women's suffrage (right to vote).

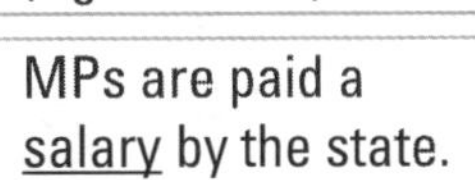

**1911** MPs are paid a salary by the state. The Parliament Act means that the House of Lords can no longer block laws passed by the House of Commons.

**1918** The Fourth Reform Act gives the vote to all men over 21 and women over 30, extending the electorate from eight million to 21 million. Women are eligible to become MPs.

**1928** Women over 21 get the vote – the same age as men.

**1945** Defeat of fascist dictatorships at the end of the Second World War leads to greater democracy in Europe and Japan p.70 ➤. The beginning of the Cold War between the democratic capitalist West and communist East.

**1948** The UN Declaration of Human Rights p.8 ➤.

**1964/5** Date of the US Civil Rights Act and Voting Rights Act: key moments in the battle for political equality for black people.

**1969** The voting age in the UK is reduced to 18.

**1989** The Fall of the Berlin Wall: the collapse of Soviet (Russian) and East European communism leads to greater democracy in these countries. Pro-democracy protests in China.

**1994** The first full election in South Africa marks the end of apartheid.

**c.1995** The use of the Internet becomes widespread pp.52–53 ➤.

**1999** The date of the Devolution of powers to the Scottish Parliament and the new assemblies in Wales and Northern Ireland p.30 ➤.

**2000** Electoral democracies account for 120 of the world's 192 countries (60% of the world's population).

## ACTIVITIES

1. **In groups of three, discuss what you think were the three most important steps on the road to full democracy. Be prepared to justify your choice in a class discussion.**
2. **Investigate your top three steps further by using the Internet and your school or local library. Prepare a section of a leaflet called 'Steps to democracy'.**
3. **The last time the voting age was lowered was in 1969, when 18–20 year olds were allowed to vote. Some people believe the voting age should be lowered again – to 16. Read the statement on Worksheet 11 and debate the issue in class.**

### Key Words

Act of Parliament • constitution
democracy • devolution
direct democracy • federal
franchise • representative democracy
separation of powers

# HOW BRITAIN IS GOVERNED

**Any government consists of three parts – the legislature, which makes the laws, the executive, which takes the day-to-day decisions to run the country, and the judiciary, the judges and magistrates who enforce the laws** pp.12–21**. This lesson considers Britain's legislature (Parliament) and executive (government ministers and civil servants).**

## PARLIAMENT

- Britain is a representative democracy. We elect MPs (members of Parliament) who represent us in Parliament
- Britain is also a constitutional monarchy. The powers of the monarch are defined by the constitution.

Parliament is made up of the House of Commons, the House of Lords and the reigning monarch. Parliament has several functions:

1. It is the legislative body of government, making laws and examining their detail.
2. It protects the rights of citizens; in particular, members of Parliament (MPs) represent the concerns and interests of their constituents.
3. It questions government ministers about their policies.
4. It holds debates on matters of national and international interest.

Queen

PARLIAMENT

House of Commons — House of Lords

### FACTFILE: HOUSE OF COMMONS

**Structure**

- Two sets of benches face each other across the floor of the chamber: one for the government, one for the opposition.
- MPs stand at the dispatch boxes in the middle, where they make speeches. The chairperson, or Speaker, keeps order from their chair behind the dispatch boxes.
- The arrangement of the chamber contributes to it being a battleground between the two main parties of government and opposition.

**Business**

- The House of Commons consists of 659 MPs, who meet for about 200 to 250 days of the year, mostly in the afternoons and evenings, with a long summer break.
- Business starts with Question Time, when government ministers answer questions from other MPs about their departments' work. Ministers may also make statements about their policies.
- Debates are held, mostly as part of the process of law-making, but also on other matters p.13. MPs shout 'Aye' or 'No' after the debate: if it isn't clear who has won, a proper vote is taken.

**Committees**

- Much of the work of the Commons is done by specialised committees, which meet in the mornings and afternoons to scrutinise government.
- Standing committees look carefully at Bills after their second reading, and suggest amendments for the House to consider at third reading.
- Select committees consider wider political issues, such as finance (the Public Finance Committee), and question ministers on their work in those areas.

## FACTFILE: THE MONARCH

### Function

- The monarch (or sovereign) plays a largely ceremonial role as head of state and symbol of the national community.
- The monarch opens each session of Parliament by reading the Queen's Speech (or King's Speech), prepared by the government, which details the programme of the new government.
- In theory, the monarch does have certain powers, e.g. she has to give approval to new laws, but the last time a monarch refused to do this was in 1707.

### Reform

- The monarchy is criticised for several reasons: he or she is unelected, socially unrepresentative, and the monarchy is expensive to maintain.
- There are therefore calls to reform the monarchy, e.g. to transfer their powers to the Speaker of the House of Commons, and to make the royal family more open and up-to-date. There are also calls to abolish the monarchy altogether, and make Britain a republic.
- However, the public are widely in favour of the monarchy. A large number are in favour of giving the Queen or King a greater role in government.

## FACTFILE: HOUSE OF LORDS

### Structure

- The House of Lords consists of about 1200 members known as peers.
- About 60% are hereditary peers who have inherited the right to sit in the Lords through their family.
- About 36% are life peers who have been appointed for their lifetime only.
- The remaining 4% are law lords (senior judges) and Church of England bishops.

### Function

- Its main function is as a second chamber, reviewing and revising the laws passing through the Commons p.13. It is prohibited from blocking any Bills for more than one year, and it cannot block any financial Bills.
- The Lords can also introduce their own Bills, which then go through the Commons in the usual way.
- It debates matters of public interest.

- It acts as the final court of appeal in the judicial system p.14.

### Reform

- No other legislative chamber in the world has members chosen by right of birth.
- In 1999, hereditary peers lost their voting rights, except for 92 who will keep this right until the next stage of reform.
- A royal commission is considering the detail of reform. The House of Lords will probably be made up of both elected and appointed members.

**Key Words**

constitution • executive • judiciary
legislature • representative democracy

## ACTIVITIES

1. In pairs, tour Parliament on www.explore.parliament.uk. Then draw up a factsheet on Britain's Parliament aimed at Year 7 pupils.
2. In groups, discuss how powerful are (a) the Queen, (b) the House of Commons, and (c) the House of Lords in the government of Britain.
3. Explain in one paragraph what you understand by the terms 'executive' and 'legislature'. Refer to Britain's government in your answer.
4. Read about the executive branch of Britain's government on Worksheet 12, and complete the activities.

# ELECTIONS AND POLITICAL PARTIES

**A general election allows people to choose their Member of Parliament. The political party that wins the most seats in the House of Commons forms the government. General elections therefore allow people to choose how they wish to be governed.**

## CANDIDATES

- British, Commonwealth or Irish Republican citizens may stand as candidates if they are aged 21 or over.
- Certain people are not qualified to stand, including members of the House of Lords, the clergy, senior civil servants, judges and members of the armed forces.
- Candidates must be nominated by ten electors living in the local constituency.
- To discourage frivolous candidates, they must pay a £500 deposit, which is lost if they don't win 5% of the votes cast.
- Candidates almost always represent one of the political parties. 'Independents'– usually single-issue campaigners – can stand but they are rarely elected.

## VOTERS

- All British citizens can vote if they are aged 18 or over. Their names must be on the electoral register of their local council. Commonwealth and Irish Republican citizens can vote if they live in the UK.
- Certain people are not qualified to vote, including members of the House of Lords, patients detained under mental health legislation and prisoners sentenced to more than 12 months in jail.
- If you are on holiday or working abroad, or if you are too ill or disabled to vote in person, you can apply for a postal vote.
- Voting is by secret ballot at a polling station. The voter marks the ballot paper with a cross against the name of their chosen candidate.
- Voting is optional. In the 2001 general election, less than 59% of the electorate voted. (Source HMSO website)

## CONSTITUENCIES

- The UK is divided into 659 areas, called constituencies (or seats). There are roughly the same number of people in each constituency (about 67000).
- Each party fighting for the seat will select one candidate to be the MP.
- Each member of the electorate lives in a constituency and has to register to vote there. The electorate then vote for the person they wish to represent them in Parliament.

## THE ELECTION CAMPAIGN

- A general election has to be held at least once every five years.
- It is up to the prime minister when to call the election. They will choose a time favourable to them.
- Sometimes a general election is forced by Parliament passing a vote of 'no confidence' in the government.
- Each party produces a manifesto outlining their policies. They also produce publicity material, transmit party political broadcasts on TV and radio, and canvass support on the streets.

# POLITICAL PARTIES

- A political party is a group of people who share roughly the same views. They work together so that they have a better chance of gaining power.
- Britain has been described as a two-party system. The first-past-the-post electoral system (the system by which the party that gets the majority of votes takes power) means that government has always alternated between two parties (since 1945 these have been Labour and the Conservatives).
- Parties have often been described as left wing or right wing depending on their overall view of society (or ideology). Left-wing parties support greater government intervention in the economy, equality of wealth and opportunity, and progressive values. Right-wing parties support freemarket capitalism, greater freedom of choice and traditional values.
- In the 1990s this left/right opposition in British politics broke down. There is now a general agreement (consensus) on the main issues – support for the market economy and a decent society with a balance of rights and responsibilities for citizens.
- The major parties differ greatly on only two main issues: European integration pp.76–77 and political reform (e.g. devolution p.30).

| | Labour Party | Conservative Party | Liberal Democrats |
|---|---|---|---|
| **Leader** | Tony Blair | Iain Duncan Smith | Charles Kennedy |
| **History** | Formed in 1900 from trade unions and socialist groups. New Labour, in power since 1997, is now more social democratic than socialist. | Developed from the Tories in the 1830s. Grew more right wing under Margaret Thatcher (prime minister, 1979–90). | Formed in 1988 from the Liberal Party and the Social Democratic Party. Excluded from power by Britain's first-past-the-post electoral system. |
| **Ideologies/ Policies** | Equality of opportunity, strengthening community, extending welfare, mixed economy | Liberty, individualism, traditional values, freedom from government controls, strong military defence | Liberty, safeguards for political and social rights, smaller role for government, electoral reform |

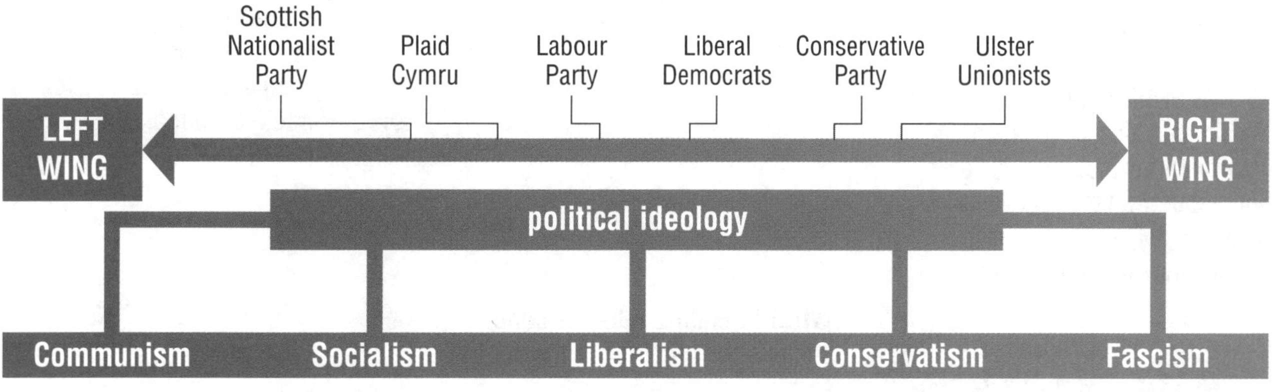


*British political parties and their ideologies*

**Key Words**
electoral reform • general election
government • political party

## ACTIVITIES

1. **Read through what you have learned about general elections, then set a quiz of five questions for your partner.**
2. **Read Worksheet 13 on electoral reform, and answer the questions there.**
3. **Look up the websites of the three main political parties (www.labour.org.uk, www.conservative-party.org.uk and www.libdems.org.uk). Compare the aims of the parties. Which party has the most appealing message?**

# REGIONAL AND LOCAL GOVERNMENT

**Since 1997 there has been a movement towards devolution in the UK, giving greater powers to the regions. This is called regional government.**
**This lesson also looks at the work of local government – a level of government even closer to the people – and asks how it could be made more democratic.**

## REGIONAL GOVERNMENT

**Until 1997 the UK was a very centralised state, ruled from Westminster. New Labour has begun a programme of decentralisation and devolution, for two reasons:**

- **to respect the needs of the different countries and regions for greater self-government**
- **to make strategic planning in particular areas more effective and accountable.**

### NORTHERN IRELAND ASSEMBLY

**WHERE:** Stormont, Belfast.
**WHEN:** 1998, after a referendum supporting the Good Friday Agreement brings peace to Northern Ireland.
**WHO:** 108 members elected by proportional representation.
Leader: First Minister.
**WHAT POWERS:** Controls education, health and local government in Northern Ireland. There is co-operation with the Irish Republic on matters of common interest, such as agriculture and transport.

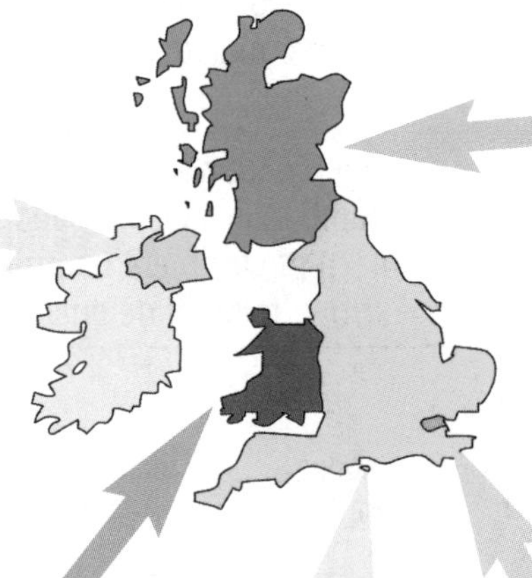

### SCOTTISH PARLIAMENT

**WHERE:** Edinburgh.
**WHEN:** Referendum, 1997 (74.3% voted Yes). First elections 1999.
**WHO:** 129 members elected by proportional representation.
Leader: First Minister.
**WHAT POWERS:** The Scottish Parliament has control over all of Scotland's internal affairs. It has the power to set taxes to pay for its programme and to make laws.

### WELSH ASSEMBLY

**WHERE:** Cardiff.
**WHEN:** Referendum, 1997 (50.3% voted Yes). First elections 1999.
**WHO:** 60 members elected by proportional representation.
Leader: First Secretary.
**WHAT POWERS:** The Welsh Assembly has a budget of £7 billion, and controls agriculture, education, economic development, health, housing and transport in Wales. It does not set taxes or make laws.

### THE FUTURE: ENGLISH REGIONS?

**WHERE:** Eight English regions, such as the north-east, the south-east and the south-west.
**WHEN:** Government proposals in 2002 suggest referendums for the regional assemblies, with the first assembly in about 2006.
**WHO:** About 25–30 members each, elected by proportional representation.
**WHAT POWERS:** Control over economic development, housing, health improvement and culture. Local councils will keep control of social services, education and other services.

### GREATER LONDON AUTHORITY (GLA)

**WHERE:** City Hall, London.
**WHEN:** Referendum, 1998 (72% voted Yes). First elections 2000.
**WHO:** 25 Assembly members and one mayor, elected in a combination of first-past-the-post and proportional representation.
**WHAT POWERS:** Controls economic development and strategic planning in London, in areas such as transport, regeneration, the environment and tourism. The GLA does not have law-making or tax-raising powers.

# LOCAL GOVERNMENT

## PURPOSE

1. Local government is an efficient method of administering local services.
2. It encourages democratic participation and citizenship by involving large numbers of people in the decision-making process.
3. Local authorities can represent the identity of a community.

## STRUCTURE

- In **Wales and Scotland** there is a single-tier (or unitary) system, in which local functions are controlled by only one layer of government. Community councils form the grassroots layer of government.
- In **England** there is a mixture of single-tier and two-tier systems. In areas with a two-tier system, functions are shared between county councils and district councils. Parish councils form the grassroots layer of government.
- Local authorities raise money for the services they provide through a mixture of central government grants, council tax, business rates and charges.

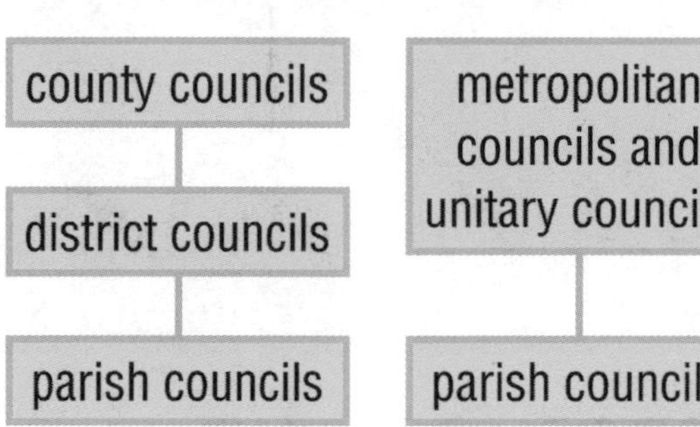


## SERVICES

Local government spends about £75 billion a year, half of which is on education and housing. They provide a wide range of services:

- Protective: police, emergency services, consumer protection.
- Environmental: roads, transport, planning, environmental health.
- Personal: education, careers, housing, social work.
- Recreational: sports facilities, museums, galleries, theatres.
- Commercial: trading services, economic development.

## COUNCILLORS

- Anyone over the age of 21 can stand for election to a local council, as long as they have some connection with the area.
- There are about 23 000 councillors in Britain, plus 70 000 parish and community councillors. A quarter spend over 30 hours per week on council duties. Most are unpaid, though they get allowances for attending meetings.
- Councillors perform different roles, such as representing particular geographical areas or groups, making policies in certain service areas and managing the delivery of services.

WALES and SCOTLAND

unitary councils

community councils

**Key Words**

decentralisation • devolution
referendum

## ACTIVITIES

1. Explain in a short paragraph what 'devolution' means. In a short paragraph, refer to what you have learned about regional government in Britain.
2. In groups, research your local council. What is its structure, what services does it provide, and who are your councillors?
3. In pairs, discuss the statements on regional and local democracy on Worksheet 14.
4. Investigate the powers that the regional government has in your own area. If there is no regional government, do you think there should be?

# CHANGING SOCIETY

**Apart from elections, what opportunities are there for ordinary people to be involved in the democratic process?**
**What changes are being made to increase democratic participation?**

## PRESSURE GROUPS

- There are thousands of pressure groups in Britain. They try to influence the government at national and/or local level by campaigning for a particular interest or issue.
- In the last 50 years, membership of political parties has declined but membership of pressure groups has increased greatly.

### TYPES

- Interest groups represent the interests of business organisations, professional organisations and trade unions p.68 ➤, e.g. British Medical Association, National Union of Students.
- Cause groups promote a particular cause or idea in religion, education, sport, the environment, welfare, etc., e.g. RSPCA, Shelter, Amnesty International, Greenpeace.
- Pressure groups can also be divided into insider groups, which are consulted by government and have a more official status, e.g. National Farmers Union, and outsider groups, which are kept at arms' length by the government, e.g. Animal Liberation Front.

### METHODS

- Pressure groups use a variety of means to achieve their goal. Most groups use peaceful methods; others use high-profile or even illegal tactics.

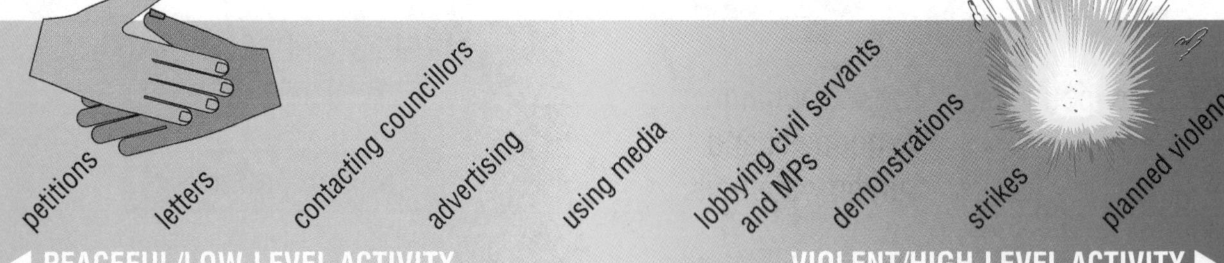


### ARE PRESSURE GROUPS GOOD FOR DEMOCRACY?

#### YES, BECAUSE ...

- ... they allow like-minded citizens to communicate and make their minority views heard.
- ... they provide a means of involvement in the democratic system and the community.
- ... they help disperse power from central institutions, and provide a check on the power of the government.
- ... They provide the government with technical expertise and advice.

#### NO, BECAUSE ...

- ... they can be thought to receive more attention than their issues warrant.
- ... they operate in a less open and accountable way than established democratic groups, e.g. by 'fixing' decisions with ministers.
- ... they apply influence from a narrow point of view rather than in the interests of society as a whole.
- ... they often have unelected leaders.

## REFERENDUMS

- One feature of direct democracy is its use of referendums to consult the public.
- There have been nearly 500 national referendums in Switzerland since 1850, and they are often used in Italy and some US states.
- In Britain referendums have been used for continuing membership of the EU (1975) and for devolution (1997–8) p.30➤. They have also been promised on the single currency p.80➤ and electoral reform p.29➤.

**FOR:** Referendums allow people to express their views directly. They consult people on important matters with far-reaching implications (mainly on the constitution). They allow a divided party or government to unite around a popular decision.

**AGAINST:** Referendums allow politicians to escape their responsibilities. Politicians expect the public to make important decisions on complex issues.

## INCREASING DEMOCRACY

*Lower and lower turnouts at elections in Britain have led to concern about a decline in democratic participation. In particular, it is thought by some that:*

- *political parties are too similar and untrustworthy*
- *local councils are just the junior partner of central government: they have no real powers or independence*
- *the decline of the trade unions has denied a forum for political participation, especially among male manual workers.*

*Various methods are therefore being used or suggested to increase democratic participation, such as:*

- *the development of e-democracy, in which national and local government bodies interact with citizens via email, websites and forums, including electronic voting*
- *the Representation of the People Act 2000 makes it easier for voters, including the homeless, those in mental institutions and remand prisoners, to register and vote*
- *the government is encouraging local councils to increase citizen involvement in the decision-making process through focus groups, opinion polls and referendums, etc. It would like mayors to act as chief executive rather than in a ceremonial role*

*Some people, however, feel that this is not enough, and that local councils should: (a) have more functions, decision-making powers and responsibility, e.g. for taxation, and (b) should all be single-tier to reduce confusion and bureaucracy* p.31➤.

**Key Words**

constitution • devolution
direct democracy • pressure group
referendum • trade union

### ACTIVITIES

1. List three pressure groups not mentioned on these pages and say what types they are.
2. In groups, discuss whether pressure groups are good for democracy.
3. Read the views on joining a pressure group and voting in elections on Worksheet 15. Discuss these in class before answering the questions on the sheet.
4. Investigate the history and use of the referendum by using the Internet and your local library. Write a factsheet about referendums aimed at Year 8 pupils.

# WHAT IS THE UK?

**What exactly is the United Kingdom, or Britain? What defines the countries and regions that make up the UK, and how important are they to your own identity?**

## NORTHERN IRELAND

**Geography:** A province of the UK consisting of six counties at the north-eastern edge of the island of Ireland. The western part is more rural and less developed than the east, which is focused on the industrial capital, Belfast. Population 1.7 million.

**History:** English monarchs tried to subdue the whole of Ireland for hundreds of years. The Catholic majority were oppressed by the Protestant minority, who were settlers from England and Scotland. Ireland was split into Northern and Southern Ireland in 1920 – Southern Ireland soon broke away from the UK to become the Republic of Ireland. In Northern Ireland, continued violence between Catholic (the minority in this region) and Protestant (majority) groups – The Troubles – eventually led to the Good Friday Agreement of 1998. This set up a devolved Assembly and allows for cross-border co-operation with the Republic p.30 >.

**Economy:** The linen and shipbuilding industries are still important, as are the engineering, chemical and service industries. Northern Ireland suffered economically during the Troubles but is now attracting much investment.

**Culture and politics:** The Catholic minority (nationalists) associate with the culture, traditions and religion of the Irish Republic. Many would like Northern Ireland to become part of a united Ireland. The Protestant majority (unionists) associate strongly with the culture of the British mainland. Most wish to remain British. Irish politics is dominated by this religious and cultural divide.

## UK ... OK?

There are several terms that relate to different parts of the British Isles, which are easily confused:

- The United Kingdom (UK) is a political term: it consists of England, Scotland, Wales and Northern Ireland. Another term commonly used for the UK is Britain.
- The British Isles is a geographical term: it consists of the two main islands of Great Britain and Ireland, and many smaller islands. Great Britain is England, Scotland and Wales; Ireland is Northern Ireland and the Republic of Ireland.

## WALES

**Geography:** Hilly/mountainous region of 2.9 million people, two-thirds of whom live in the southern valleys and coastal areas. A quarter of Wales is a National Park or Area of Outstanding Natural Beauty. Its capital is Cardiff.

**History:** A Celtic stronghold, eventually brought under English rule by Edward I in 1282. Two Acts of Union under Henry VIII incorporated Wales into England. The Welsh narrowly voted for a national assembly in 1997, providing limited self-rule p.30 >.

**Economy:** The coal industry has almost disappeared, but the steel industry remains important, along with other manufacturing, e-commerce and tourism. Overseas and UK investment is aiding economic regeneration.

**Culture:** A distinctive culture based on Wales's Celtic roots, nonconformist religion and the Welsh language. A fifth of the population say they speak Welsh, though it is the first language only in the rural north and west. Welsh literature is one of the oldest in Europe.

**Politics:** Mainly Labour, with Plaid Cymru (the nationalist party) as the main opposition. Plaid Cymru aims to preserve the Welsh culture, language and economy rather than campaign for an independent Wales.

# SCOTLAND

**Geography:** The northern part of Great Britain, population 5 million, divided into highland (mountainous) and lowland areas. Much wild and unspoilt landscape, including many of the UK's mountains. Main cities are Edinburgh (the capital), Glasgow, Dundee and Aberdeen.

**History:** Scotland remained a separate kingdom from England in the Middle Ages (Robert the Bruce defeated Edward II of England in 1314). The two kingdoms came together in 1603 when James VI of Scotland also became James I of England. The two countries agreed on a single parliament at London in 1707. A new Scottish Parliament, giving some degree of self-rule, was set up in 1999 p.30 ►.

**Economy:** Once based on coal, steel and shipbuilding, the economy now extends to offshore oil and gas fields, and high-tech industries and financial services.

**Culture:** Scotland has had its own legal, educational and Presbyterian church system for hundreds of years. The Gaelic and Scots languages are being revived but are spoken by only a small proportion of the population. The media focuses on Scottish affairs and supports the idea that Scotland is different from England.

**Politics:** Mainly Labour, challenged by the Scottish Nationalist Party (SNP). The SNP wants Scotland to be fully independent from England and believes that the devolved National Parliament is not enough.

# ENGLAND

**Geography:** The southern part of Great Britain, mainly lowland but with upland regions in the north and south-west. Its population is 50 million and its capital is London. Although 80% of the population live in towns of over 10 000 people, England has many unspoilt rural and coastal areas.

**History:** The name 'England' is derived from 'the Angles', one of the German tribes that settled after the Romans left p.37 ►. The last successful invasion of England was by the Normans in 1066. England absorbed Wales in the 16th century, and formed a union with Scotland in 1707.

**Economy:** The economic performance of the nine English regions varies a great deal. The south-east is the richest region; other regions qualify for EU funding.

**Culture:** Although the English regions are very varied, they share a rich history, language, literature and artistic and architectural heritage. The Church of England is the established church (the official religion).

**Politics:** In 2001 the Labour Party kept their large majority in the House of Commons, with the Conservative Party as the opposition. Unlike the other regions of Britain, England does not have a separate elected national body p.30 ►.

## Identifying with the regions

An opinion poll in 1998 asked people in Great Britain where their loyalties were strongest.

very strong · fairly strong · not very strong · not at all strong · don't know

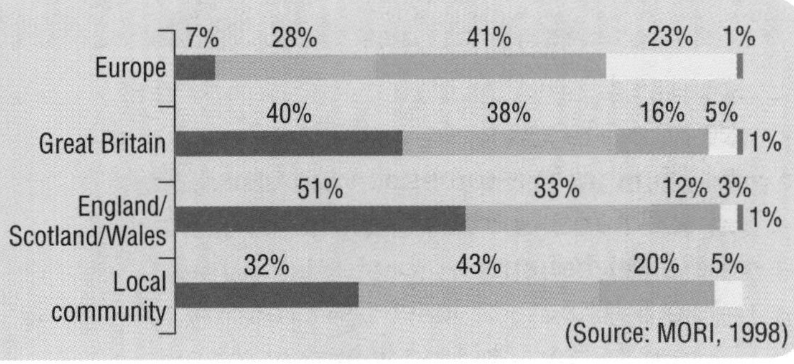


## ACTIVITIES

**Key Words**
devolution • nationalist

1. **Why is the United Kingdom called the United Kingdom?**
2. **Describe the region where you live. Illustrate your description by cutting out some pictures of the landscape and famous places from your region.**
3. **Research the history of your local area. To find out how it has changed, ask local residents, use libraries or the Internet. Take some photographs to highlight the history and culture of your local area.**
4. **Look at the columns in the first question on Worksheet 16. Write numbers 1 to 10 in the columns, depending on how strong you feel your loyalties are (10 = strongest loyalty/identity). Compare your columns with a partner's, then complete question 1 on the worksheet.**

# WHERE DO WE COME FROM?

**People have come to Britain from many different countries over thousands of years. They brought their <u>culture</u> with them – their language, religion and way of life. Together these cultures have combined to form the <u>multicultural</u> society that we know today as Britain.**

## To Britain from the World

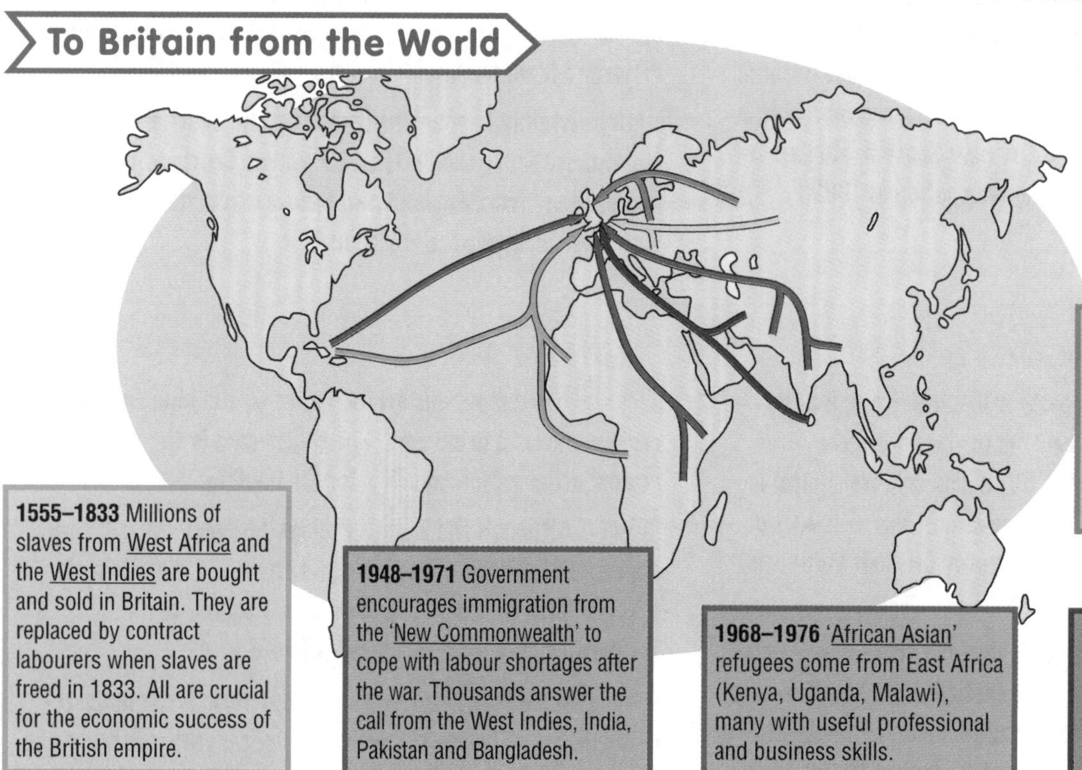

**1000–150 BCE** <u>Celts</u> arriv from Russia via Central Europe. Their language and culture is still strong in Scotland, Wales and southwest England.

**1870–1914** 120 000 <u>Russian</u> and <u>Polish Jews</u> flee to Britain, settling in London, Leeds and Manchester. They specialis in the clothing, shoemaking and furniture trades.

**1555–1833** Millions of slaves from <u>West Africa</u> and the <u>West Indies</u> are bought and sold in Britain. They are replaced by contract labourers when slaves are freed in 1833. All are crucial for the economic success of the British empire.

**1948–1971** Government encourages immigration from the '<u>New Commonwealth</u>' to cope with labour shortages after the war. Thousands answer the call from the West Indies, India, Pakistan and Bangladesh.

**1968–1976** '<u>African Asian</u>' refugees come from East Africa (Kenya, Uganda, Malawi), many with useful professional and business skills.

**2003** <u>Asylum seekers</u> continue to seek a haven in Britain from persecution an war in such countries as Sri Lanka, Iraq and Afghanistan

## IMMIGRANTS AND REFUGEES

### IMMIGRANTS

An <u>immigrant</u> is someone who travels to another country in order to live there permanently.

- Some choose to leave their country to seek better jobs and living conditions (<u>economic migrants</u>).
- Some are forced to flee their country through hunger, persecution or war (<u>political migrants, refugees</u>; see right).

Immigrants have often been seen as a threat to the host community, even though they bring diversity and skills. Some groups have <u>integrated</u> into the host community by accepting their values. Others have tried to <u>hold on</u> to their religion and culture.

### REFUGEES

- A <u>refugee</u> is someone who has fled to a new country because they fear persecution as a result of their beliefs, religion, race or culture.
- An <u>asylum seeker</u> is a refugee who is applying for protection (asylum) in a foreign country for their own safety. The right to asylum is laid down in Article 14 of the Universal Declaration of Human Rights.
- Those seeking asylum in the UK come here from a <u>range of countries</u>. Many of the countries have oppressive regimes or are afflicted by civil war. In 2000 the highest number of asylum applications came from refugees from Iraq, Sri Lanka, Yugoslavia, Afghanistan, Iran and Somalia.

## To Britain from Europe

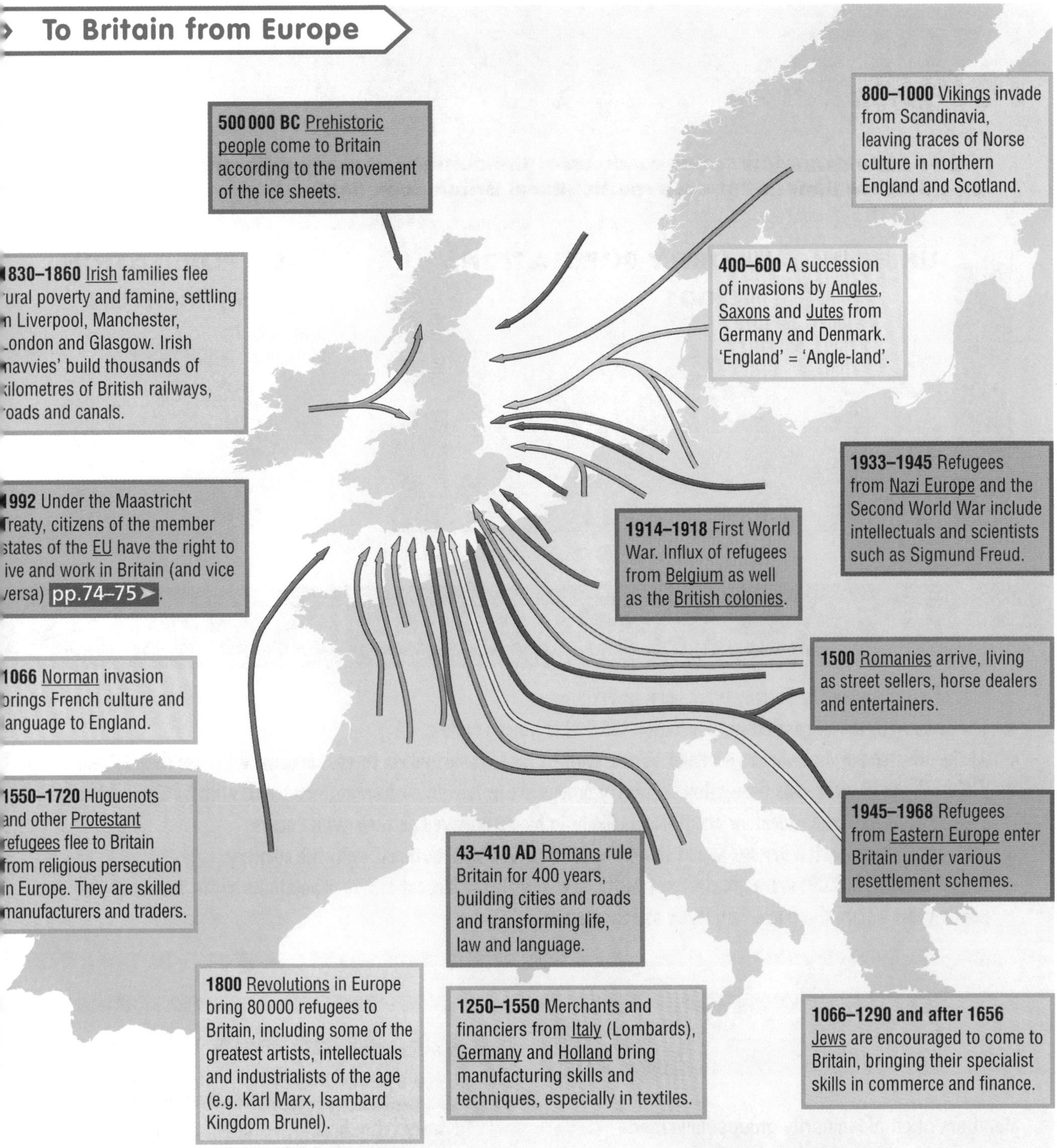

**500 000 BC** Prehistoric people come to Britain according to the movement of the ice sheets.

**800–1000** Vikings invade from Scandinavia, leaving traces of Norse culture in northern England and Scotland.

**1830–1860** Irish families flee rural poverty and famine, settling in Liverpool, Manchester, London and Glasgow. Irish 'navvies' build thousands of kilometres of British railways, roads and canals.

**400–600** A succession of invasions by Angles, Saxons and Jutes from Germany and Denmark. 'England' = 'Angle-land'.

**1933–1945** Refugees from Nazi Europe and the Second World War include intellectuals and scientists such as Sigmund Freud.

**1992** Under the Maastricht Treaty, citizens of the member states of the EU have the right to live and work in Britain (and vice versa) pp.74–75➤.

**1914–1918** First World War. Influx of refugees from Belgium as well as the British colonies.

**1066** Norman invasion brings French culture and language to England.

**1500** Romanies arrive, living as street sellers, horse dealers and entertainers.

**1550–1720** Huguenots and other Protestant refugees flee to Britain from religious persecution in Europe. They are skilled manufacturers and traders.

**43–410 AD** Romans rule Britain for 400 years, building cities and roads and transforming life, law and language.

**1945–1968** Refugees from Eastern Europe enter Britain under various resettlement schemes.

**1800** Revolutions in Europe bring 80 000 refugees to Britain, including some of the greatest artists, intellectuals and industrialists of the age (e.g. Karl Marx, Isambard Kingdom Brunel).

**1250–1550** Merchants and financiers from Italy (Lombards), Germany and Holland bring manufacturing skills and techniques, especially in textiles.

**1066–1290 and after 1656** Jews are encouraged to come to Britain, bringing their specialist skills in commerce and finance.

### Key Words

asylum seeker • diversity
immigrant • multicultural
refugee

## ACTIVITIES

1. **List three reasons why immigrants have come to Britain, and two ways in which Britain has benefited from immigrants.**
2. **Log on to www.traceit.com and enter your family name. What can you discover about the history of your family name? What do you think this means about your own roots?**
3. **Do you view today's immigrants and asylum seekers differently when you see them as the latest chapter in a long history of immigration to the UK? Write one paragraph, giving your reasons.**
4. **Read the factsheet on Britain's refugees and asylum seekers on Worksheet 17. Then answer the questions that follow.**

# MULTICULTURAL BRITAIN

**A multicultural society is one made up of the cultures of many different ethnic groups or religions. What does multicultural Britain look like?**

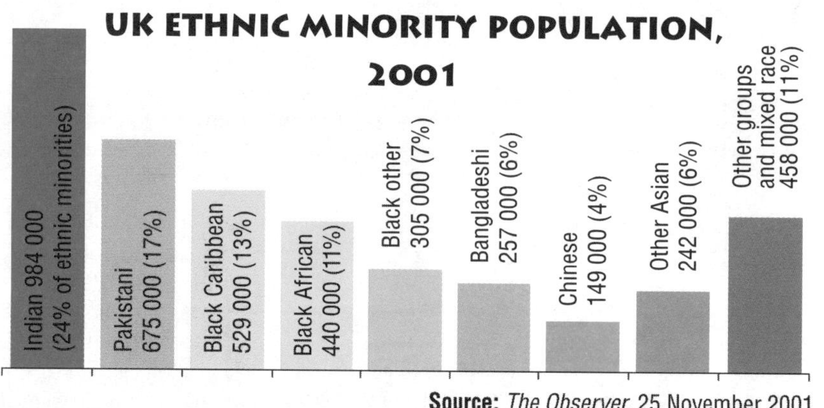


**Source:** *The Observer*, 25 November 2001

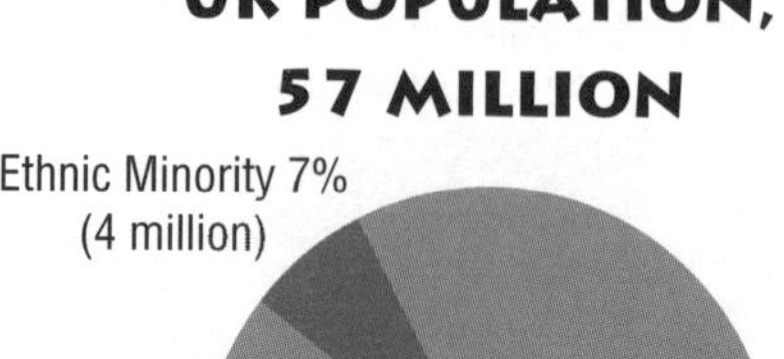


## SOME FACTS ABOUT RACE IN BRITAIN

- Half of ethnic minority Britons were born in Britain.
- The area with the largest ethnic population (33.9%) is Inner London.
- At the other end of the scale are Scotland, Wales, south-west England and north-east England with less than 2% each.
- 71% of 16- to 19-year-olds from ethnic minority groups are in full-time education, compared with 58% of whites.
- Those not in full-time education are twice as likely to be unemployed as their white peers.
- 56% of ethnic minority Britons live in the 44 most deprived local authorities in the country.
- Racial tensions in 2001 were greatest not in the areas with the largest ethnic populations but in towns in the north-west where there are high levels of segregation.

## BRITAIN'S BENEFIT

Members of ethnic minority groups have made important contributions in many areas of British life.

### Enterprise

E.g. Two-thirds of small shops supplying sweets, tobacco and newspapers are owned by Asians. They stay open late and on Sundays and provide great service to the local community.

### Industry

E.g. Over a quarter of London Underground's staff belong to ethnic minorities. A third of London's black cabs are owned and run by Jewish people.

### Skills

E.g. A quarter of Britain's doctors were born overseas. In the 1970s it was calculated that each of these doctors saved Britain £28 000 in training.

Immigrants bring fresh views and new ways of doing things.

Many have brought skills and qualifications that the host country has needed.

Many have been enterprising, setting up businesses and providing jobs in the local community.

Many have been willing to do jobs that others have not wanted to do.

### Cultural influence

E.g. Chinese and Indian restaurants and takeaways have become an essential part of eating out in Britain. Italian, Bangladeshi, Cantonese, Greek and Thai restaurants also do a roaring business.

Many other areas of British life have benefited from ethnic minority involvement, including sport and entertainment.

# RELIGIOUS DIVERSITY

- Christianity has been the most popular faith in Britain for hundreds of years. The Church of England is the official (established) church, but there are many other Christian churches.
- Most of the other world religions are also practised in Britain, especially in the large cities where ethnic minorities have settled (see table). Britain in the 21st century is a multifaith society.
- Everyone in the UK has the right to religious freedom. Schools must teach Christianity and take into account the teachings and practises of the other main religions.

| Religion | Membership | Origin of most members |
|---|---|---|
| Hinduism | 350 000 | India (Gujeratis), East Africa |
| Judaism | 350 000 | Eastern Europe |
| Islam (Muslim) | 850 000 | Pakistan, East Africa |
| Sikhism | 440 000 | India (Punjabis) |

(Source: ICM)

*The main non-Christian faiths practised in Britain. There are smaller groupings of Buddhists, Baha'is, Jains and Zoroastrians.*

# A MATTER OF OPINION

**An ICM poll in 2001 asked people to choose one of the following statements:**

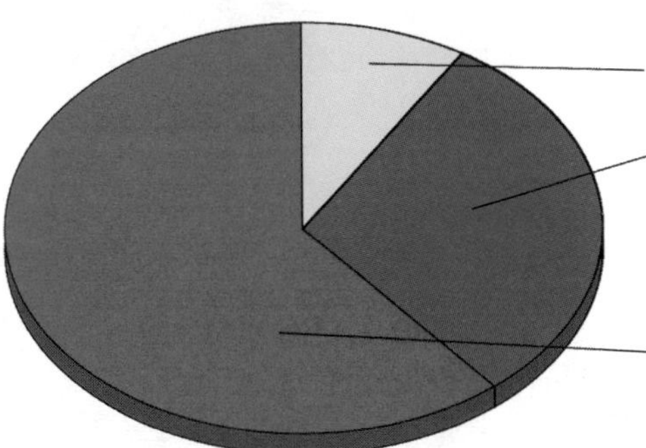

**To be truly British it is necessary to be white. 9%**

**People from ethnic minorities need to demonstrate a real commitment to this country before they can be considered British. 30%**

**As long as an individual feels British they are British, regardless of colour. 61%**

**Most people therefore feel that colour is not an important factor in defining Britishness.**

## Key Words

diversity • ethnic minority • multicultural

## ACTIVITIES

1. **Discuss the bar chart and the 'facts about race' on page 38 with a partner. What do you find most interesting or surprising?**
2. **(a) Write down three advantages of a multicultural society. (b) Explain what is meant by 'diversity'. Why do many people think that societies benefit from diversity?**
3. **Produce a restaurant menu reflecting Britain's multicultural society. Label each dish with the ethnic or cultural tradition from which it comes.**
4. **Carry out a survey in your local area of the variety of different ethnic groups and religions that make up the community. Include shops, places of worship, clubs, etc.**
5. **Read the interviews on Worksheet 18 (My Britain). Answer the questions that follow.**

# PREJUDICE AND DISCRIMINATION

**Prejudice is judging people on the basis of stereotypes, without proper knowledge or thought.**
**When prejudice results in treating someone unfairly, this is called discrimination. For discrimination due to gender and disability, see 'Equal Opportunities at Work'** pp.64–65 >**. This lesson focuses on racial discrimination.**

## THE UPS AND DOWNS OF RACE RELATIONS IN BRITAIN

**1948** – The first West Indian immigrants arrive on *SS Empire Windrush*. They are accused of taking jobs from local people, even though they came to Britain because of labour shortages.

**1958** – Riots take place at Notting Hill and Nottingham, provoked by white racists.

**1962** – The Commonwealth Immigration Act restricts immigration from the 'New Commonwealth'. The Act is racist as it distinguishes non-white from white immigrants.

**1976** – The Race Relations Act is passed to tackle racial discrimination and promote racial equality. The Commission for Racial Equality is set up.

**1980/81** – Riots in Bristol, London, Liverpool and elsewhere are sparked by heavy-handed policing in immigrant areas.

**1993** – Stephen Lawrence is stabbed to death by a gang of white youths in south London.

**1999** – The MacPherson inquiry into Stephen Lawrence's death criticises 'institutional racism' in the police. This begins the process of positive change in other public bodies as well, and leads to a widening of the Race Relations Act.

**2001/2** – Racial tensions follow the 11 September attacks on America. Increased numbers of asylum seekers also trigger racist feelings.

## ACTIVITIES

**Key Words**
discrimination • institutional racism • prejudice

1. **What is the Race Relations Act? How has it been strengthened recently?**
2. **'Although life has improved in many ways for ethnic minorities in Britain, racial discrimination and harassment are still too often daily experiences for many people.' Discuss this, with reference to some of the facts and figures on these two pages.**
3. **Do you agree that racist attacks should be treated more seriously than other forms of violence? Give reasons for your answer.**
4. **Read the case studies on Worksheet 19 and answer the questions.**

# RACIAL DISCRIMINATION – THE LAW

- The Race Relations Act 1976 bans racial discrimination in employment, education, service industries and housing. It is an offence for a person or an institution to treat someone less favourably because of their race, either directly or indirectly.
- An amendment passed in 2000 extended the Act so that it covered the public services (police, hospitals, local councils, etc). These now have the duty to promote racial equality.
- The Commission for Racial Equality, set up in 1976 to check that the Race Relations Act was working, now has wider powers, including taking public bodies to court.
- The Act does not cover discrimination on the grounds of religion. However, Sikhs and Jews have been defined as racial groups for the purposes of the Act.
- Racially–motivated violence or threats of violence (racial harassment) are covered by the criminal law, although some people think racial harassment should be a specific offence.
- Once they have been admitted to Britain, immigrants and their children have the same rights and privileges in law as other citizens. There is no second-class citizen status, as exists in some European countries for immigrant workers.

**Racial discrimination can be both direct and indirect.**

- It is direct discrimination if someone is treated less favourably than another on grounds of their race or ethnic background, e.g. if you are refused a job because you are black.
- It is indirect discrimination if a rule or policy puts people from a particular racial or ethnic group at a disadvantage, e.g. if workers are not allowed to wear anything on their head. Unless the company can justify this rule on grounds other than race, it is unlawful.

# DISCRIMINATION IN BRITAIN: THE FACTS

**Ethnic minorities are often the most deprived in our society. They have low expectations of public services, especially the police, the courts, local councils and the immigration services. Poverty, poor education, poor housing and unemployment are barriers to racial harmony in Britain.**

### EDUCATION

- In 1999 only 30% of Pakistani pupils, 37% of black pupils and 30% of Bangladeshi pupils achieved five or more GCSEs at grades A*–C, compared with 50% of white pupils and 62% of Indian pupils.
- African-Caribbean pupils are nearly six times more likely to be excluded than white pupils, although they are no more likely to truant than white pupils.

### HEALTH

- People from ethnic minority groups are more likely to suffer ill health.
- Infant mortality is 100% higher for the children of African-Caribbean or Pakistani mothers than white mothers.

### HOUSING

- 70% of people from ethnic minority groups live in the 88 poorest local authority districts, compared with 40% of the general population.
- 40% of Bangladeshi and Pakistani families live in overcrowded housing.

### LEGAL SYSTEM

- The Home Office has accepted that there may be 130 000 racially-motivated crimes each year, including racial abuse and attacks on people and property.
- In 1998/9 black people were six times more likely to be stopped and searched by the police than white people.
- People from ethnic minorities make up 18% of the male prison population and 24% of the female prison population.

### WORK

- In 1998, 13% of people from ethnic minorities were unemployed, compared with 6% of white people.
- African male graduates are seven times more likely to be unemployed than white male graduates.

# CHANGING SOCIETY

**What opportunities are there for individuals and groups to promote the values of a multicultural society?**

## WHAT GROUPS CAN DO...

There are hundreds of national and local (and international) groups dedicated to promoting race relations in Britain, educating about racial prejudice and campaigning against racial discrimination.

### ME TOO

www.metoo.org.uk › go

INFO

The campaigning group Me Too was formed in reaction to the racist nail bombings in London in 1999.

AIMS

1 To encourage everyone to make a united statement of support for any minority which suffers violence, and to wear the 'me too' badge as a symbol of that solidarity.
2 To widen the campaign into an educational forum providing materials on the themes of tolerance, diversity and co-operation.

### REFUGEE COUNCIL

www.refugeecouncil.org.uk › go

INFO

The British Refugee Council, formed in 1981, is an independent charity which works with asylum seekers and refugees. It is financed by government, the EU, trusts and members.

AIMS

1 To give advice and support to asylum seekers and refugees and their communities.
2 To offer training and employment courses so that asylum seekers can use their skills in Britain.
3 To campaign for the voice of refugees and asylum seekers to be heard by government and society.

### OPERATION BLACK VOTE

INFO

Operation Black Vote is a non-party-political campaign, founded in 1996. It is supported by a coalition of mainly black organisations.

AIMS

1 To get the black community to play its full part in Britain's democracy, e.g. by urging black people to register to vote.
2 To show politicians what it means to be black in Britain, to force them to address the inequality of opportunity that black people suffer.
3 To promote the cultural diversity of British society in the best interests of society as a whole.

### KICK IT OUT

www.kickitout.org › go

INFO

Kick It Out is football's anti-racism campaign. It was started by the Commission for Racial Equality and the Professional Footballers' Association in 1993.

AIMS

1 To challenge racism at all levels of the game, from professional to amateur.
2 To encourage local ethnic minority communities to participate in the game, and particularly to end the exclusion of Asians.
3 To develop resources for young people in schools, colleges and youth organisations.

# WHAT YOU CAN DO...

There are many ways in which you can take a stand against racism.

**Problem.**
You are being abused or attacked because of your race, colour, nationality or ethnic background, or you witness someone else being harassed.
**Action.**
Report it to the person in charge (manager, teacher) or to the police, your local Racial Equality Council, Citizen's Advice Bureau or law centre.

**Problem.**
You find a newspaper article, TV or radio programme, or advertisement racially offensive.
**Action.**
Write to the newspaper, TV or radio station. In addition, complain to the Press Complaints Commission, the Radio Authority, the Independent Television Commission or the BBC's Listener and Viewer Relations section. For adverts, complain to the Advertising Standards Authority p.47.

**Problem.**
You are worried about racial discrimination in an organisation or at work.
**Action.**
Report it to your manager, and inform your trade union if you have one. You can also contact your local Racial Equality Council, Citizens' Advice Bureau or the Commission for Racial Equality.

**Problem.**
You want to work for racial equality in your area.
**Action.**
Contact your local Racial Equality Council – the address will be in the phone book – or look up:

www.cre.gov.uk/about/recs.html › go

## ACTIVITIES

**Key Words**
discrimination • diversity
prejudice

1. **Research your school's anti-bullying policy. Does it include a section on racist bullying? Discuss with a partner whether you think it is effective and what you could do to improve it. Then share your views with the class.**
2. **Read the advice on putting a stop to racist abuse (Worksheet 20) and answer the questions.**
3. **'I see racist behaviour all around me, but there's nothing I can do about it, is there?' (Mike) Write a reply to Mike.**
4. **Look up the websites of the four organisations described opposite.**
   **(a) What are their latest campaigns?**
   **(b) What opportunities are there for people to support the organisation?**
5. **Contact your local Racial Equality Council (look up www.cre.gov.uk/about/recs.html) and find out what it is doing to promote racial equality and harmony in your area.**

# WHAT IS THE MEDIA?

**The term 'media' refers to the means of communication that exist in the world. The mass media, in particular, have a huge influence in society.**

## THE MASS MEDIA

### TELEVISION

| Types | Broadcast area | Who pays? | Who's in charge? |
|---|---|---|---|
| Public sector (BBC) | National | Users, via an annual licence fee | The Director General reports to a board of governors appointed by the government |
| Commercial sector (ITV) | National (Channels 4 and 5) and regional (Channel 3) | Advertisers and sponsors | Private companies: the Chief Executive reports to a board of directors |
| Satellite and cable (BSkyB, etc.) | National | Advertisers and sponsors | Private companies: the Chief Executive reports to a board of directors |

- The BBC's charter states that it must make programmes that 'inform and entertain' – they don't have to have as much majority appeal as the programmes produced by commercial stations.
- The digital TV revolution will mean a huge increase in the number of TV programmes and improved technical quality. The government plans to complete the process by 2010.

### RADIO

- BBC Radio runs five national stations (Radios 1 to 5) and many regional stations.
- Commercial radio stations are given licences by the Radio Authority to run national and regional stations such as Virgin FM and Talk Sport.
- Community radio stations are given a restricted service licence (RSL) to broadcast to a specific group, e.g. a youth organisation or a hospital.
- Pirate radio stations operate illegally (without licences). There are also a growing number of Internet radio stations.

### NEWSPAPERS

| Type | Format | Style | Readership | Circulation | Examples |
|---|---|---|---|---|---|
| Tabloid | Small | Less formal, lighter weight | Mainly working class | 20.6 million/day | *Sun*, *Mirror* |
| Broadsheet | Large | More formal, serious coverage | Mainly middle class | 5.7 million/day | *The Times*, *Guardian* |

- Three-quarters of the adult population read one of the ten daily and nine Sunday newspapers.
- Readership has declined since about 1960 through competition from TV.

### THE INTERNET

A vast network of computer links which allows millions of people to exchange information across the world pp.52–53 >.

# A SHORT HISTORY OF THE MEDIA

c. 3400 BC — Earliest writing known, in Sumeria (Middle East).
c. 60 BC — First newspapers record senate meetings in ancient Rome.
c. 750 AD — Wooden blocks first used for printing, in China.
c. 1450 AD — Johann Gutenberg invents the printing press.
c. 1600 — Political communication is mainly verbal, in small groups and large public meetings. Some broadsheets and pamphlets produced.
1785 — The first issue of *The Times*, the first proper daily newspaper in Britain.
1876 — Alexander Graham Bell invents the telephone.
1895 — The first radio signals are broadcast by Guglielmo Marconi.
1925 — John Logie Baird transmits a television picture by radio waves.
1936 — The BBC transmits the first public TV service.
c. 1960 — Television becomes the most popular form of media in Britain.
1989 — Launch of Sky satellite TV.
c. 1995 — Widespread use of the Internet in Britain.

# THE ROLE OF THE MEDIA IN A DEMOCRACY

The mass media are an essential part of modern democracy. According to the pluralist view, the media provides a 'free market of ideas':

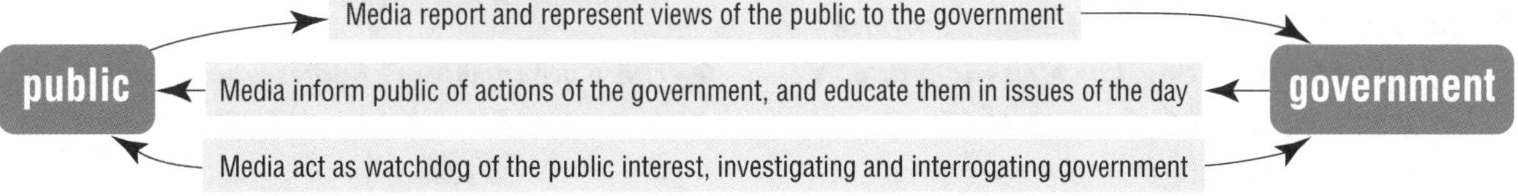


Some people criticise the pluralist view and prefer to define the above from a dominance view, in which the 'market of ideas' is not free but distorted by powerful interests:

- 80% of newspaper circulation is in the hands of four large corporations p.51.
- Most media organisations have to make a profit, which affects their output. Material is more likely to be based on personalities, revelations and disasters.
- In the lobby system, political journalists receive special briefings from government spokesmen (spin doctors), allowing the government to dominate the agenda p.46.
- The government can put pressure on the BBC, especially during wartime.

## ACTIVITIES

**1. Discuss what you understand by the term 'mass media'. Why is it such an important aspect of society?**

**2. In groups, list all the reasons why you watch TV. Share this list in a whole class discussion.**

**3. Explain in one paragraph what the pluralist view is of the role of the media in a democracy.**

**4. Read Worksheet 21 on the media and answer the questions.**

# CONTROLLING THE MEDIA

**One important feature of a democracy is that there should be a free flow of information so that its citizens are properly informed. But this flow is controlled to a certain degree by actions of the state and regulatory bodies.**

## THE POWER OF THE STATE

*Officially there is no censorship in a democracy – the media is free to broadcast and print the information that they want. However, there are several ways in which the output or content of information is controlled in Britain.*

- *The Official Secrets Act 1989 makes it illegal to release information harmful to the public interest, in the areas of security, defence, international relations and crime. Critics say that the definitions of 'harmful' are too broad and vague.*
- *Other laws prevent or discourage the media from publishing material that is obscene, libellous or an invasion of privacy.*
- *The BBC is committed to the public service model of broadcasting, in which radio and TV programmes must be accurate and fair, as well as educate, inform and entertain.*
- *D-notices (Defence Notices) are requests from the government to newspaper and TV journalists not to run stories that are harmful to national security.*
- *The government uses the media to market their philosophies. The lobby system ensures that only certain journalists are given information by the government. Spin doctors release the information at the best time and present it in the best way.*
- *There are regulatory bodies which control the content and the activities of different parts of the media* p.47 ➤.

## FREEDOM OF INFORMATION

The government has recently been trying to reverse the 'culture of secrecy' that makes Britain one of the most secretive states in the Western world. There is now an 'open government' website with information about government departments: www.ukonline.gov.uk The Freedom of Information Act was passed in 2000, though it will not take full effect until 2005.

- For the first time there will be general access to information held by public authorities. Exceptions are made to protect the public interest.
- Public bodies such as the police, health authorities, schools and prisons have to provide information about their performance and conduct.

Critics of the Act say that it is too weak, that:

- there are too many exclusions from the Act, e.g. factual information on which policy decisions are made
- although a new information commissioner can order disclosure in the public interest, a cabinet minister can veto (cancel) the order.

# REGULATING THE MEDIA

**Different bodies regulate the content of different parts of the media. Currently there are several organisations that regulate broadcasting. However this is changing. One of the regulators, the ITC, is going to be absorbed by the New Office of Communications (OFCOM), which will shortly take over its responsibilities.**

iTC
Independent Television Commission
PUTTING VIEWERS FIRST

Press Complaints Commission

| | The press | Advertising (non-broadcast) | Broadcasting |
|---|---|---|---|
| **Regulator(s)** | Press Complaints Commission (PCC) – an independent body of 16 people. | Advertising Standards Authority (ASA). | Independent Television Commission (ITC), Broadcasting Standards Commission (BSC), Radio Authority. |
| **Powers** | The PCC decides whether a paper has broken the industry's code of practice, e.g. over privacy, accuracy and treatment of children and other groups. | The ASA ensures that all advertisements follow the industry's code, and are 'legal, decent, honest and truthful'. | They ensure that TV and radio programmes are fair, decent and appropriate to the time they are broadcast. They can fine offenders and force them to issue apologies. |
| **Big issue** | The PCC has been criticised (a) because it is made up of members of the newspaper industry, (b) its powers are too limited – it cannot fine newspapers. | In 2001 the ASA resolved 12 500 complaints about 10 000 adverts. 650 adverts had to be changed or withdrawn. However, the advertising industry has huge power over the press as they provide it with so much money. | The government is creating an Office of Communications (Ofcom) in 2003 which will replace these bodies. This will provide a one-stop shop for dealing with complaints, and provide basic rules for all broadcasters to follow. |

## ACTIVITIES

1. **Explain what is meant by 'censorship'. Can censorship be justified in certain circumstances?**
2. **In pairs, decide which of the following (if any) you think should be regulated in the media, and which should be banned: (a) stories about the private lives of celebrities, (b) pornography, (c) photographs and stories of those who have suffered a tragedy, (d) unfair treatment of different groups, e.g. ethnic minorities, (e) swearing. Does your view change depending on the form of the media?**
3. **Why is freedom of information important for democracy? Log on to Charter 88's website for further information (www.charter88.org.uk).**
4. **In pairs, read the Independent Television Commission's code of practice for advertising and children (Worksheet 22).**

# REPRESENTING SOCIETY

**What effect does the media have on its audience? Does it merely report and represent society as it is?**

## THE EFFECTS OF THE MEDIA

There are different theories about the effect that the media has on an audience. These disagree about which is the more powerful force – the media or the audience.

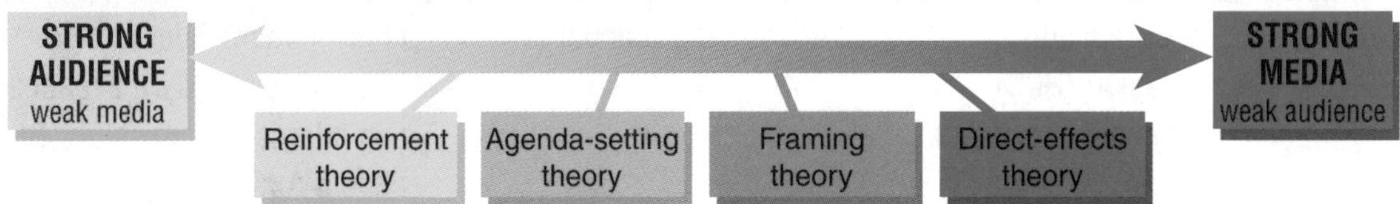


Reinforcement theory claims that the media has little effect on its audience.

- The media reinforces existing opinions rather than creating opinions in the audience.
- Market competition ensures that the media gives the audience what they want, rather than what the media wants.
- There are different media with different messages: we select to suit our opinions and tastes.

Agenda-setting theory claims that the media has a limited effect on its audience:

- The media sets the agenda: it doesn't tell people what to think, but tells them what to think about.
- The media's influence lies in selecting which issues to cover and bring to public attention.
- The media highlights certain issues and brings them to the public's attention, e.g. political sleaze, road rage, football hooligans.

Framing theory also claims that the media has some effect on its audience:

- The media affects how the public thinks about issues and how it reacts to events.
- It does this by framing issues – interpreting and presenting them in certain ways p.50 ➤.
- To provide human interest, the media trivialises issues and emphasises style and personalities.

Direct-effects theory claims that the media has a strong effect on the audience:

- The media affects not just what people think about, but the way in which they think about it.
- TV encourages its audience to be passive receivers of information and opinions.
- Violence in TV programmes and videos influences people's behaviour.
- There is some evidence to suggest that newspapers influence the voting patterns of their readers.

## STEREOTYPES IN THE MEDIA

The media has been accused of using stereotypes which reinforce people's prejudices about certain groups in society.

- Television soap operas, dramas and comedies have to establish characters quickly, and use stereotypes as short-cuts. The need for snappy sound bites has the same effect in the other media.
- All sorts of people and groups are stereotyped in this way, including women, gays, children, the police, the elderly and business people.
- Culture and class stereotypes are also used, e.g. ethnic minorities are almost never portrayed as being as powerful or as rich as the white majority.
- Absence from the media is another form of stereotyping. For example, young people with disabilities are rarely shown on TV or in films except to highlight the issue of their disability.

# DANGERS OF STEREOTYPING



- ***Stereotyping affects the power and place in society of the groups that are stereotyped. For example, if black groups are under-represented in the media, or represented in negative terms, this both alienates them and increases prejudice against them.***
- ***Stereotypes not only reinforce prejudices but can also encourage violence against certain groups. Propaganda in Nazi Germany encouraged the persecution of Jews and homosexuals in this way.***
- ***Stereotyping can lead to the creation of folk devils and moral panics. Media focus on child killers, drug users, paedophiles, video nasties and unhealthy food may have created such moral panics.***

## CREATING A MORAL PANIC

**1** Concern develops over a group of citizens, who appear to threaten society's values or interests.

**2** The media turn the group into a folk devil and report the issue in a simplistic and exaggerated way.

**3** Public 'knowledge' of the group increases, so more examples are reported to the media and police, and fear is increased.

**4** Public reaction becomes hysterical – a moral panic fuelled by media overreaction and stereotyping.

**5** Politicians, police and judges introduce harsher measures against the original group.

**Key Words**

media • stereotype

## ACTIVITIES

1. In groups, discuss whether you think the media or the public is more powerful, or whether there is a balance between the two (see page 48). Choose a spokesperson to report on your views in a class discussion.
2. Collect some stories or reports from national newspapers which affect your opinion in different ways (e.g. a strong effect or no effect). Does this exercise lead you to support any of the four theories about the effects of the media (see page 48)?
3. Make a WANTED poster for a TV stereotype (Worksheet 23) and complete the exercises.

# BIAS IN THE MEDIA

**If the media is to fulfil its role in a democracy, it should be unbiased. But how fair and balanced is it? Ownership, the market and party politics are all factors that influence the media in important ways.**

## BIAS IN THE PRESS

Newspapers are not required by law to be balanced and impartial. On the contrary, there are several reasons why they have a tendency to be biased.

1 The press is controlled by rich owners and multinationals which have particular interests, especially business interests p.51 >.
2 Press barons have always wanted power, which often means controlling the editorial policy of their papers.
3 Newspapers rely heavily on advertising income: they have to be careful not to offend the businesses that fund them.
4 Newspapers want to carve out a media market which makes them distinctive from their main rival, television.

The British press is far more party political than the press in most other western countries.

- Until 1997 most newspapers supported the Conservative Party, especially the mass-market tabloids *Sun*, *Mail* and *Express*. The *Sun* claimed it was responsible for the defeat of the Labour Party in the 1992 general election.
- The *Sun* switched support to Labour in 1997; some people think this contributed to Labour's landslide victory. Others think that most people already knew what they were going to vote, so the newspaper's influence was small.

## BIAS IN THE BROADCAST MEDIA

- Television and radio are required by law to be balanced. Most people trust both the BBC and the ITV news.
- Equal airtime is offered to each of the main political parties at election times.
- However, governments of both parties often complain that the BBC is biased against them.
- The Glasgow Media Group and other social scientists claim that television news is systematically biased towards conservative values.
- Others prefer the term mediation to bias, as the representation of news is determined by various 'filters'.

## MEDIATING THE NEWS

Mediation refers to the 'skewing' of news stories in subtle or unintentional ways.

- Use of language: the choice of words gives the audience very different impressions, e.g. terrorists/freedom fighters, overran/liberated, insist/plead.
- Use of images: these reinforce the message. Are the demonstrators shown looking angry and violent, or oppressed by the police?
- News values: different values determine whether a story is selected in the first place. Bad news, conflict and personality stories tend to win over other issues.
- Self-censorship: news editors will not even attempt to run certain stories if they know they will not be acceptable to the business or other interests of the owners and/or advertisers.
- Limited sources: media corporations concentrate their resources on where major news stories are likely to happen, and accept stories from only a few 'trusted' sources.

# OWNERSHIP

In recent years ownership of the media has become more concentrated. There are dangers in this.

- It weakens media pluralism and competition, preventing a full variety of views from being expressed.
- It results in huge organisations having great amounts of power but little accountability or responsibility.

## THE PRESS

About 80% of newspaper circulation is in the hands of four large corporations:

- Associated Newspapers (owning the *Daily Mail*, *the Mail on Sunday*)
- Mirror Newspaper Group (owning the *Mirror*, *Sunday Mirror*, *Sunday People*)
- United Newspapers (owning *Express*, *Sunday Express*, *Star*, *Standard*)
- News International (owning *The Times*, *Sunday Times*, *News of the World*, *Sun*).

These press barons also own much of the regional press and have strong TV interests, e.g. News International owns Sky TV. Multimedia conglomerates include newspapers, journals, books, radio, TV, entertainment and other business interests, often across the world p.82 >.

## TV AND RADIO

- The broadcast media fit the pluralist model of the media more easily, as there is a clearer distinction between ownership and control p.45 >. The BBC is owned by the government but run by an independent board of governors.
- However, the ownership of independent television is becoming more concentrated. The 2002 Communications Bill proposes relaxing controls, which would allow a single company to operate all of the ITV network for the first time.

## HOWEVER ...

Modern technology has also led to a different trend – for the media to become increasingly specialised and pluralist.

- There are an increasing number of magazines and other publications.
- *The Independent* broadsheet newspaper has survived since its launch in 1986, despite being politically independent.
- Local and community radio is growing rapidly.
- The Internet allows individuals instant access to an enormous variety of sources of information pp.52–53 >.

**Key Words**

bias • mass media

## ACTIVITIES

1. 'To fulfil its role in a democracy, the media should be as unbiased as possible.' 'But as long as the bias is obvious, then it's harmless.' Continue this discussion.
2. In pairs, list the headlines of today's front-page stories in all the tabloid newspapers. Why were these stories selected? Do you think they are the most important issues of the day?
3. Video the evening news or look at the stories in an issue of a national newspaper. List the places where you think the news is being 'mediated', and give your reasons.
4. In pairs, look at the extracts from the newspaper reports that your teacher will give you (Worksheet 24).

# CHANGING SOCIETY

**The Internet originated as an American project in the 1960s to enable computers at universities, research centres and the defence industry to share resources. It now has about 600 million users worldwide, of which two-thirds are in Europe and North America. The Internet has already made huge changes to society, but people are divided as to whether those changes are for good or ill.**

## ADVANTAGES OF THE INTERNET

### ACCESS TO INFORMATION

- The development of digitalisation means that all kinds of information can be stored, manipulated and transmitted quickly and cheaply.
- There is a vast amount of material on the Internet and it is growing at a fantastic rate.
- You can work or communicate from anywhere as long as you have a computer and a phone line p.63 ➤.

### EMPOWERING THE COMMUNITY

- The Internet makes e-democracy possible, so that people have better access to public services and can make their views heard, including in elections p.33 ➤.
- Special interest groups with limited resources can publish information and co-ordinate campaigns using the Internet.
- The Internet can help remove barriers such as sex, age, race and disability – we are all equal in cyberspace.
- The Internet has also broken down geographical barriers, contributing to the process of globalisation pp.82–83 ➤.

### BUSINESS AND COMMERCE

- Online shopping and e-commerce are major growth areas of the Internet.
- Businesses can respond quickly to customers' needs, advertise widely, enter new markets, conduct business transactions and make huge savings in time and expense.
- Customers can shop and bank on the Internet, saving time, effort and money. Online shopping provides immediate access to huge numbers of outlets worldwide.

### CREATIVE OPPORTUNITIES

- The Internet has provided a new medium for writing, broadcasting and entertainment.
- Messages on the Internet can be generated in many new and imaginative ways.
- The Internet has generated countless jobs in computer and information-related industries.
- The Internet allows us to relate to new people, and in new ways.

# DISADVANTAGES OF THE INTERNET

### SECURITY

- Many people are distrustful of shopping online, especially with credit cards, as information can easily be intercepted.
- Governments are concerned about terrorists using the Internet to co-ordinate their activities and attack public services.
- Children are easily exposed to the large amounts of pornography and other offensive material on the Internet, and even to dangerous contact through chatting online.

### CYBER-CRIME

- Hackers breach the security measures of computer systems belonging to governments or companies and alter records, gain confidential information or steal money.
- It is easy to break copyright laws by distributing texts, pictures, music and software around the world digitally.
- Malicious people spread huge numbers of viruses to infect others' computer systems, or waste their time by spreading hoax viruses.

### A LOAD OF RUBBISH?

- The small amount of useful information is outweighed by mountains of rubbish. It is often difficult to find what you need.
- There is a lot of inaccurate, misleading and harmful information on the Internet because it is easy to publish material on the web.

### INTERNET INEQUALITIES

- People cannot benefit from the Internet if they cannot afford the equipment, or if the infrastructure where they live is inadequate.
- As the Internet plays an ever-increasing role in society there is a danger of creating two tiers: the onliners and the offliners.
- This problem is repeated on a global scale, as the world is divided into the computer-literate and the computer-illiterate countries.

### THE GLOBAL PICTURE

- In 2002, 634 million people worldwide had Internet access.
- Non-English-speaking online users overtook English-speaking users in 2000. Two-thirds of the world's online population are now non-English speakers (mainly Asian and European languages).
- 45% of the English-speaking population had Internet access in 2002, compared with only 7% of the non-English-speaking population. However, that situation is predicted to change rapidly (see graph).

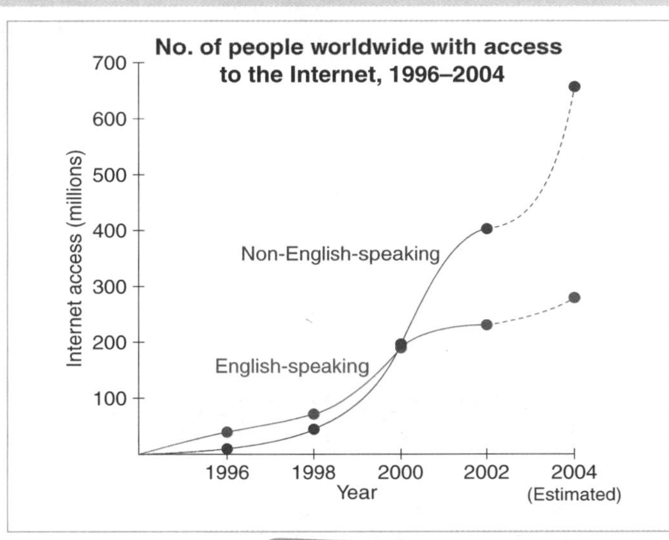


**Key Words**

democracy • globalisation
media

## ACTIVITIES

1. **Write down what you think are the two greatest advantages and the two greatest disadvantages of the Internet. Share your list with a partner – do you agree?**
2. **'The Internet is a force for democracy and more active citizenship.' Discuss this statement.**
3. **In groups, compare how your parents or carers control your access to the Internet. Is this control necessary? Is it successful?**
4. **Look at the newspaper headlines about the Internet on Worksheet 25. In pairs, discuss what the issue is in each case and why it is important. Then share your views in a class discussion.**

# THE ECONOMIC SYSTEM

**The economy of a country is the way in which goods and services are produced, distributed and consumed.**

## HOW THE MONEY GOES ROUND

In the simplest model of the economy (see below), businesses produce goods or offer services (1). They pay their workers a salary (2). The workers and their families use this money to buy goods and services (3). The shops use the money they receive to buy the goods from the businesses (4).

Growth in the economy occurs when people save money in banks (5), which is injected into businesses in the form of a loan or investment (6). The businesses use this to buy new equipment, hire or train workers, do research, etc., to create new or improved services that people want (see below).

**Simple model**

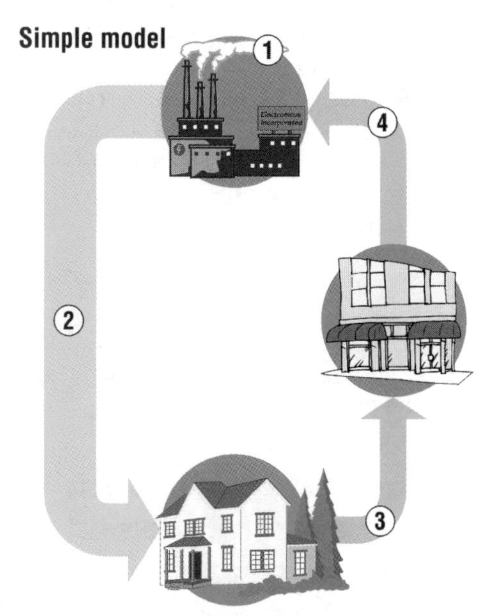


**Growth model**

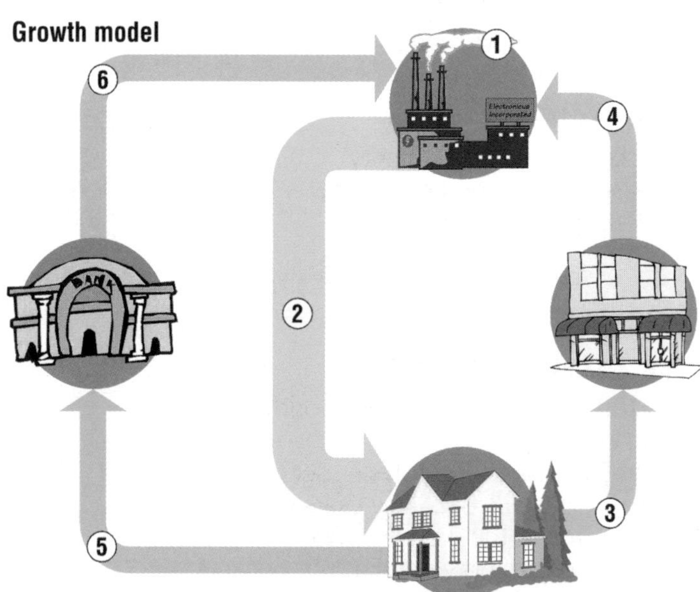


## ECONOMIC RESOURCES AND GROWTH

The economy's goods and services are produced by using different resources (called factors of production):

- **Natural resources** – businesses use the land directly (e.g. agriculture), build on it, buy or rent it, or extract raw materials from it (e.g. mining, North Sea oil).
- **Labour** – businesses need to employ people. Those who want to work and those who want to employ them together make up the labour market.
- **Money** (capital) – businesses need to invest money in machinery, buildings, workers and other resources.
- **Technology** – businesses use technology to produce goods and services more efficiently, and to find ways of producing new goods.

Improvement in any or all of these factors of production means improved productivity (the amount produced per worker), which leads to economic growth.

# ECONOMIC SYSTEMS

- In traditional economies, which are family based, people produce only as much as they need for themselves, using methods that have always worked. Money is not important.
- Free market economies are about using money to buy and sell in an open market. Activity is determined by supply and demand. The profit motive encourages enterprise and entrepreneurs (risk-takers).
- In a planned (or central) economy, all decisions about who produces what, and at what price, are made by the state. Resources are owned by the state on behalf of the people (public ownership).

## THE MIXED ECONOMY

Most countries now have mixed economies, which means they are part free market (private sector) and part planned by the government (public sector).
In a mixed economy there is a balance between the free market and the planned sectors. This balance determines how the resources are allocated:

### FREE MARKET (PRIVATE) SECTOR

The free market (private sector) provides freedom for people to choose to buy what they want, a greater range of products, opportunity for profit and growth, and greater competition which keeps prices down.

Resources are owned by private individuals and businesses.

Disadvantages are that it can encourage inequalities and greed.

### PLANNED (PUBLIC) SECTOR

The planned public sector, such as state education and the NHS, provides basic services that are available to all regardless of people's ability to pay. Their purpose is to provide an efficient, fair and safe service rather than to make a profit.

Resources are owned by the state.

Disadvantages are that public services can be inefficient, bureaucratic and lack choice.

**Key Words**

free market economy
mixed economy • planned economy
private sector • public sector

## ACTIVITIES

1. In groups, discuss what role each of the following groups play in the economy: (a) workers, (b) consumers, (c) businesses, (d) investors.
2. (a) Define the terms 'public sector' and 'private sector'. (b) Find the 'jobs vacant' section in your local newspaper and list three examples of vacancies in each sector.
3. Answer the three questions on Worksheet 26 about your local economy.

# TYPES OF BUSINESS

**Businesses lie at the heart of the economy. They can be defined in many ways, such as what sector they belong to and how they are organised.**

## HOW BUSINESSES ARE ORGANISED

### Sole traders

**WHAT?** Sole traders are businesses owned and run by one person – the sole trader or proprietor. He or she can employ others, but doesn't have to share the profits.

**WHO?** Most businesses in the UK are sole traders, such as small high-street shops, caterers and other services, and craftspeople such as carpenters and plumbers.

FOR: Easy to set up and run. Only a small amount of capital (money) needed. Control and profit kept in the hands of one person: the owner is the boss.

AGAINST: Can be difficult to raise money from a bank for expansion. Proprietor has unlimited liability for bad debts, which means he or she may have to use their own wealth to settle such debts. The boss has all the responsibility.

### Partnerships

**WHAT?** A partnership is formed when between two and 20 people jointly own and control their business. The partnership agreement outlines who has responsibility for what, and how they share the profits.

**WHO?** Partnerships are common in the professions, e.g. accountants, doctors, insurance brokers, lawyers.

FOR: Decision-making and responsibility is shared. Partners can pool different specialist skills. More capital can be raised.

AGAINST: Trusting your partners is an issue. Disputes between partners can occur. If the partnership fails, all partners are liable for the debts (unless they form a limited liability partnership).

### Limited companies

**WHAT?** A limited company is owned by its shareholders – people who have invested money in it so as to benefit when the company makes a profit. Shareholders elect a board of directors who control the company. They have limited liability for business debts (up to the size of their shareholding).

**WHO?** Smaller businesses (whose names end in 'Ltd', for 'limited liability') are private limited companies. Limited companies, which wish to raise larger amounts of money, can offer their shares to the general public on the Stock Exchange and set up a public limited company (Plc).

FOR: Limited companies have greater continuity as they do not end with the death of their shareholders – the company is a separate legal entity. People are attracted to becoming shareholders because they know exactly how much money they risk losing. Plcs can raise huge amounts of money for investment.

AGAINST: The separation of ownership and control means that the shareholders and directors may have different views on how the company should be run and what its objectives should be. Plcs are expensive to set up, and whoever started the company can lose control in a takeover bid.

### Other businesses

- A co-operative is a business that is owned collectively and managed for the economic benefit of all.
- A franchise sells a product supplied by a major supplier. The franchisee supplies the capital, and in return gets training, the brand name and support from the franchiser.
- Public corporations are owned by the state and supply goods and services to the whole economy.
- Transnational corporations have their headquarters in one country but carry out operations in many other countries as well pp.82–83.

# THE FOUR INDUSTRIAL SECTORS

**Every business in the economy belongs to one of four industrial sectors: primary, secondary, tertiary and quaternary. Each sector has a different function (see table).**

| Sector | Function of business | Examples of businesses |
|---|---|---|
| Primary | Extracting raw materials from natural resources | Coal mining, agriculture, fishing |
| Secondary | Manufacturing: turning the raw materials into finished goods | Cars, steel, clothing industries |
| Tertiary | Providing services to help people use the goods | Health, transport, tourism, catering, insurance services |
| Quaternary | Inventing new products and ideas, and managing the flow of information | Research labs, inventors, universities |

**The British economy has been dominated by each sector in turn over its history (see below).**

Before the Industrial Revolution, most economic activity involved agriculture (primary sector).

Manufacturing industry reigns supreme (secondary sector, e.g. shipbuilding and steel industries).

1700 1800 1900 2000

The Industrial Revolution – the economy depends increasingly on the secondary sector (building ships, spinning cotton to make clothes, manufacturing machinery).

Many manufacturing industries collapsed in the 1980s. The tertiary and quaternary sectors now account for 70% of output, manufacturing for 28% and agriculture for only 2%.

**Key Words**

limited company
partnership • sole trader

## ACTIVITIES

1. Explain the following terms: (a) sole trader, (b) partnership, (c) limited liability, (d) shareholder.
2. Get into pairs. One of you is a trainee carpenter, the other a trainee builder. Discuss what the advantages and disadvantages are of setting up as a partnership rather than as sole traders when you finish your training.
3. In groups, choose the best descriptions of shops in the area where you live (question 1, Worksheet 27). Discuss privatisation in your area and answer question 2 on the worksheet.

# RUNNING THE ECONOMY

**The government has been described as the biggest business in Britain. Like any business, it has to balance its income and expenditure. In April each year the Chancellor of the Exchequer sets out how the government is going to do this in the budget. The government also has the responsibility of steering the economy of Britain.**

## SPENDING MONEY

*The money spent by central and local government is called public expenditure. This provides different kinds of goods and services for the public:*

- *providing social security, by paying unemployment and other benefits*
- *funding nationwide services, such as health, defence and education*
- *running or funding public corporations and bodies, such as regional development agencies and the BBC.*

*The bar chart below shows some of the main areas of government spending (with examples in brackets).*

Government spending, 2001/2002, showing the total amount spent and the percentage annual change since 1997.

|  |  |  |
|---|---|---|
| Education (teachers, schools, universities, books) | £50bn | ▲ +4% |
| NHS (hospitals, doctors, nurses) | £60bn | ▲ +5% |
| Social security (benefits and pensions) | £110bn | ▲ +1.9% |
| Defence (army, navy, air force) | £24bn | ▼ -1.1% |
| Transport (roads, rail and bus services) | £11bn | ▼ -0.1% |
| Law and order (police, prisons, courts) | £23bn | ▲ +4.5% |

## RAISING MONEY

The main source of government income is taxation.

- Direct taxes are taxes based on earnings. They are levied (raised) directly on an individual or organisation. The main direct taxes are income tax and national insurance, both of which are calculated as a proportion of an individual's earnings.
- Indirect taxes are taxes based on spending. They are levied on goods and services. They do not relate to the amount that people earn, but stay at a fixed rate. The main indirect taxes are VAT, set at 17.5%, and excise duties, put on fuel, alcohol and cigarettes.

The pie chart below shows in more detail what taxes the government raises, and what proportion they form of the total revenue.

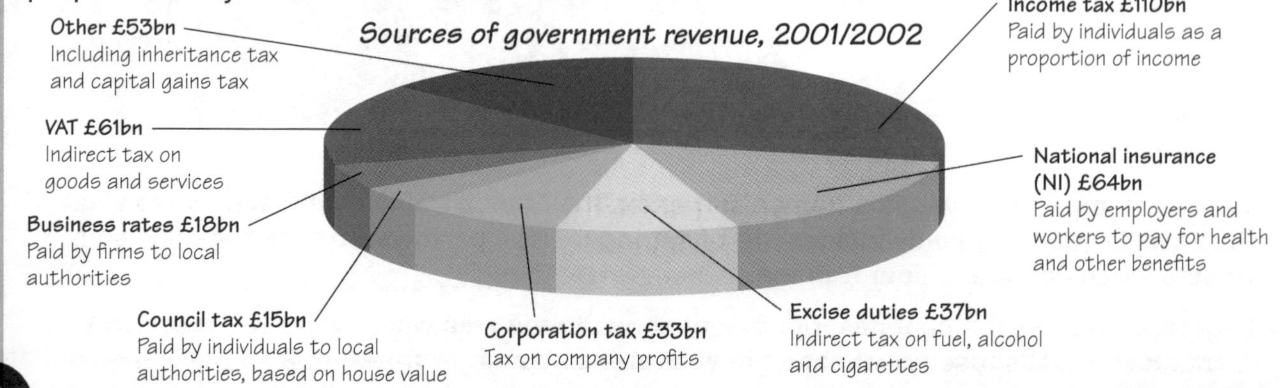

# STEERING THE ECONOMY

The government also has responsibility for steering the whole of the UK economy. It does this in several ways:

**Fiscal policy** – This is how the government raises and spends money to influence business and consumers. For example, in the 2002 budget the Chancellor announced a huge increase in spending on the NHS. Increases in spending expand the economy because they create more jobs. If the economy expands too much, however, it can result in inflation. The Chancellor therefore also raised the National Insurance rate by 1%. This squeezed the economy, as it dampened down individuals' spending.

**Monetary policy** – This is the inflation target set by the government – that is, the rate at which prices can rise. Interest rates, however, the system by which the inflation target can be met, are controlled by the Bank of England, an independent body.

**Exchange rate policy** – The government buys and sells pounds on the international market to control the value of British currency abroad. This affects the prices of goods that are imported and exported, and therefore affects inflation.

**Supply-side policies** – This refers to attempts to increase the number and skills of workers in the economy to improve the competitiveness of business. Examples are privatisation, government-sponsored training schemes, grants and tax incentives.

The UK economy is also hugely affected by the EU and international trade pp.75, 82 >.

## ACTIVITIES

1. Look at the bar chart on page 58. (a) Which are the areas of greatest government expenditure? Why do you think this is so? (b) What do the percentage annual changes since 1997 tell you about the government's spending priorities?
2. Look at the pie chart opposite. What can you learn from it about how the government raises money?
3. Write down three important ways in which the government influences the country's economy.
4. Imagine you are the Chancellor of the Exchequer. If you wanted to increase spending in three areas, which would they be? How would you raise the money – by taking it from other areas and/or raising taxes? Write a paragraph detailing your plans for the economy.
5. Complete the personal budget table on Worksheet 28 and answer question 1. Discuss this as a class. Answer questions 2 and 3 on the worksheet, giving examples of taxes and examining the costs of a wedding or having a credit card.

# CHANGING SOCIETY

- **Stakeholders are people who have an interest in a business or enterprise. This means not only that the business affects them, but also that they have some influence over how the business conducts its affairs.**
- **The UK economy is rapidly becoming a stakeholder economy: people are encouraged to participate in the economy as well as merely benefiting from it.**
- **The diagram on these pages shows how many groups of people have an interest in the activities of every business – these groups are stakeholders in business.**

## BUSY BUSINESS LTD

### OWNERS

The shareholders of a limited company own the business, and own the profits of the business. They therefore have an interest in the financial success of the business. They also have the opportunity to control the way the business is run by voting for particular directors and policies at the company's AGM (annual general meeting).

Entrepreneurs may wish to start and own a business in order to create a new product or service.

### EMPLOYEES

The workers and managers who are employed by the business are all interested in keeping their jobs to maintain or improve their income and standard of living. They also want a good environment in which to work, training to develop their skills, and to feel proud of their business (ethical/environmental issues).

Employees may also be shareholders or take part in profit-sharing schemes. Their contribution to the business is a major factor in its success or failure.

## CUSTOMERS

Customers have an interest in the business because they buy the firm's goods or use its services. They want the goods to be sold at a fair price, and may have views on ethical or other aspects of the business. They can express their views as part of a consumer group, or other pressure group pp.10–11 ➤. They can also withdraw their support altogether by not buying the product.

# LENDERS

Lenders (or creditors), such as banks, have lent the business money, so they expect to receive a return on their investment. They will get this in the form of interest payments on their loan. Banks will refuse to extend loans to businesses if they think there is little chance of the business succeeding. They will refuse to invest in expansion projects for the same reason.

# SUPPLIERS

Suppliers are the groups who provide: the buildings and equipment that the business uses; the raw materials or component parts that go to make its goods; or the goods themselves for resale (the producer or wholesaler). They are interested in the success of the business because it provides them with income.

# COMMUNITY

Businesses affect the community in many ways, both positive (providing jobs for local people, investing in the community) and negative (polluting the environment). Social responsibility is an increasingly important factor for businesses, especially for large firms with a high profile. Individuals can affect certain business decisions, such as whether a firm sets up in an area, by putting pressure on their local council, or by forming local pressure groups p.32➤.

Local government benefits from businesses, as they pay business rates which finance local services. They have certain controls over local businesses, such as refusing planning permission.

Central government benefits from a strong economy, which includes profitable businesses. The government protects other stakeholders through employment and consumer laws.

## ACTIVITIES

**1. State briefly what is meant by the term 'stakeholder'.**

**2. Discuss how the following stakeholder groups benefit from the success of a local business: (a) consumer, (b) owner, (c) supplier.**

**3. What influence do each of the following stakeholder groups have on the success or activities of a local business: (a) lender, (b) employee, (c) local community?**

**4. Discuss as a class the views on work experience (Worksheet 29). Answer the question on 'good' and 'bad' work experience.**

# A WORKING LIFE

**Working adults in the UK spend more hours working than they do any other activity. There are therefore a vast number of rules and regulations governing the world of work.**

## BASIC RIGHTS AT WORK

A person's rights at work depend on (1) laws passed by Parliament (their statutory rights) p.13 >; and (2) their contract of employment. Trainee or casual workers have the same employment rights as other employees.

All the rights described below are statutory rights. The contract of employment cannot take away these rights, although it can increase them, e.g. by allowing more holiday or pay.

## STARTING WORK

- All part-time and full-time workers have a contract with their employer. This gives both employer and employee rights and obligations, e.g. the employee has the right to work at their job and be paid, and the employer has the right to give reasonable instructions to the employee.
- The contract lists the terms and conditions of employment, such as pay, holidays and job description. The contract can be agreed verbally, but employees have the right to a written statement of the main terms of employment within two months of starting work.
- There is no such thing as a 'probationary period': statutory rights begin from the first day at work.

## LOSING YOUR JOB

- Dismissal means losing your job because of your behaviour. You can only be sacked on the spot for gross misconduct (e.g. theft). Otherwise, after one month's employment, you must be at least given one week's notice for each year of employment (up to 12 weeks). You can claim for wrongful dismissal by taking your case to an employment tribunal, which may compensate you and give you back your job p.15 >.
- Redundancy means losing your job because your employer no longer needs the job done. You have a right to redundancy pay if you have worked for the employer for at least two years. If you think you have been unfairly chosen for redundancy, you can claim for wrongful dismissal.

## HEALTH AND SAFETY

- According to the Health and Safety at Work Act, employers must take care of their employees, which includes maintaining equipment so that it is safe.
- Employers must check on the health and safety of employees who use computer screens, which may include arranging eyesight tests.
- Employees must work responsibly and follow safety procedures.

# DIFFERENT WORKING PATTERNS

Although most workers are employed full time by others, there are many different patterns of work.

- Part-time work has increased significantly over the past few decades. There are nearly as many women who work part time as full time p.64.
- Self-employed people sell their labour direct to the customer. This can mean hard work and long hours, but the possibility of greater freedom, challenge and fulfilment p.56.
- New technology means that more office jobs are being done at home, called teleworking, benefiting both employers and employees.
- People who do voluntary work in the community, for charities, hospitals and schools, etc., earn no money but improve the quality of people's lives pp.69, 91. This also applies to unpaid work in the home, such as caring, cooking and housework.

## PAY

- All employees are entitled to be paid, even if there is no work for them to do. The rates of pay will be agreed between the employer and the employee; this may be based on an agreement between the employer and the trade union p.68.
- Employers must not discriminate in the amount that they pay their workers pp.64–65.
- Since 1999 most workers aged 18 or over are entitled to the national minimum wage. In 2002/3 the minimum wage for 18- to 21-year-olds was £3.60; for 22-year-olds and over it was £4.20.

## HOURS

- Hours of work are usually agreed between the employer and the employee.
- The Working Time Regulations mean that employees cannot be forced to work for more than 48 hours per week (calculated as an average over 17 weeks). They also have the right to minimum rest breaks.
- Certain workers are not covered by these regulations, e.g. doctors in training, transport workers and the armed services.

## TIME OFF

- Full-time employees have the right to at least four weeks' paid holiday per year, according to the Working Time Regulations. Part-time workers have a proportionate amount of paid leave. However, employees must have worked for at least 13 weeks; public holidays may be included in the four weeks; and certain workers are excluded (see 'Hours').
- There is a legal minimum rate of sick pay, though an employee's contract may give more than this.
- Employees are also entitled to time off for other reasons, e.g. family emergencies, parental leave, maternity leave pp.64–65 and study/training for 16- to 17-year-olds.

## ACTIVITIES

1. In pairs, create a list of the most important health and safety regulations in school. Share your list in a class discussion.
2. Discuss the following patterns of work with a partner, then decide together on one advantage and one disadvantage for each: (a) self-employment; (b) part-time work; (c) working from home.
3. Complete the 'True or False' quiz on employees' rights and answer the questions (question 1, Worksheet 30), then give definitions of terms.
4. Investigate the Working Time Regulations by using a search engine on the world wide web. Draw up a leaflet explaining in simple terms the rights that UK workers have under these regulations.

# EQUAL OPPORTUNITIES AT WORK

- **Equal opportunities means that everyone should have the same chance to achieve a specific goal, whether that is a promotion at work, a place at university or access to healthcare. Most inequality is related in some way to discrimination** pp.40–41 >**.**
- **It is illegal for employers to discriminate against anyone on the grounds of their gender (sex), race or disability. (There is no law protecting a person against discrimination for their sexual orientation.)**
- **This lesson looks at inequalities in employment on the basis of gender and disability.**

## PREGNANCY AND MOTHERHOOD

European Union directives on maternity leave and pay were issued in the 1970s and 1980s, but only recently formalised in English law.

- From 2000 pregnant employees have been entitled to 18 weeks' maternity leave without pay. Extra leave can be taken depending on length of service.
- Statutory maternity pay is also available for a total of 18 weeks.
- From 1996 women have had the right to paid time off both before and after the birth of their child.

Forward-thinking businesses encourage flexible working patterns to suit employees' commitments to their families, e.g. flexitime, job-sharing, teleworking and homeworking p.63 >.

## WOMEN AT WORK

## SEX DISCRIMINATION

The Sex Discrimination Acts 1975 and 1986 make it unlawful to treat anyone, because of their sex, less favourably than a person of the opposite sex.

- Direct discrimination means treating a women less favourably than a man (or vice versa), e.g. not employing someone because she is a woman.
- Indirect discrimination means applying conditions equally to both sexes, but which favour one sex over another, e.g. not employing someone because they may take time off to have a baby.

Sexual harassment is a form of direct discrimination. It covers a wide range of things, e.g. repeated and unwanted verbal or sexual advances, leering and physical contact.

## EQUAL PAY

- The Equal Pay Act states that women are entitled to the same pay as a man doing either the same (or similar) job or a job of equal value.
- The Act covers all pay, e.g. bonuses, holiday pay, sick pay and pensions, not just wages and salaries.
- It covers most UK workers, whether they are on full-time, part-time, casual or temporary contracts.

## WORKING PATTERNS

Although more and more women are working, there are still great inequalities between the sexes in the workplace. Women's work is concentrated in part-time, lower skilled and lower paid jobs, with less access to training (see graphs and table).

*Percentage of jobs held by women over 100 years*

| | 1900 | 2000 |
|---|---|---|
| Legal profession | 0% | 28% |
| Medical practitioners | 0.5% | 31% |
| Nurses, midwives, etc. | 99% | 92% |
| Housekeepers, cleaners, etc. | 93% | 85% |
| General labourers | 0.5% | 8% |

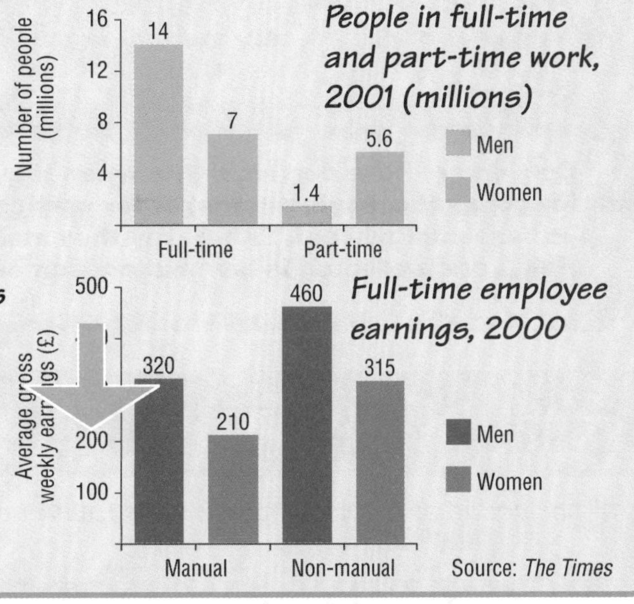


## DISABILITY AT WORK

The Disability Discrimination Act was passed in 1995. It protects 8.5 million people with disabilities against discrimination in employment and access to goods, services and housing.

- Under the Act, firms of 15 or more employees must not treat people with disabilities less favourably in terms of recruitment, pay, promotion or other terms of employment.
- From 2004 all businesses and organisations have to adjust their premises, where reasonable, to overcome physical barriers to access.

## FIGHTING DISCRIMINATION

If you feel that you are the victim of discrimination:

1 Try to sort things out personally and informally.
2 If this is unsuccessful, get advice from your Citizens' Advice Bureau, law centre or trade union.
3 The Equal Opportunities Commission deals with complaints about sex discrimination; the Disability Rights Commission deals with complaints about disability discrimination. Both bodies will help you take your case to an employment tribunal, but they have limited enforcement powers themselves p.15.

**Key Words**

contract • discrimination
equal opportunities

## ACTIVITIES

1. In pairs, look at the graphs and table at the top of the page. (a) What do they tell us about the different status between men and women in the workplace? (b) How can you explain these differences?
2. Write down two main features of each of the equal opportunities laws: (a) the Sex Discrimination Act, (b) the Equal Pay Act, (c) the Disability Discrimination Act.
3. In small groups, read the case studies on Worksheet 31 and discuss whether the employer is breaking the law in each case.
4. Use one of the following websites to describe the help that the organisation offers to victims of discrimination: (a) the Equal Opportunities Commission (www.eoc.org.uk), (b) the Disability Rights Commission (www.drc-gb.org), (c) the Citizens' Advice Bureau (www.nacab.org.uk).

# CONSUMERS' RIGHTS

**Consumers have certain rights when they are shopping. Consumers may be shopping for goods (i.e. buying items) or for services (i.e. buying a skill such as a haircut or professional advice). Either way they make a contract with the trader. Consumers' rights are protected in law; but consumers have responsibilities too** p.69 >.

## YOUR RIGHTS WHEN SHOPPING

If the goods or services supplied are faulty or inadequate, your rights are protected in law.

### WHEN BUYING GOODS ...

Under the Sale of Goods Act the law says that the goods must be:

- **of satisfactory quality** – taking into account the description and price.
- **fit for their purposes** – they must do what the seller and manufacturer says they can do.
- **as described** – they must fit the description on the package or display sign, or that given by the seller.

This law applies also to second-hand goods, goods in a sale, and goods bought by mail order, over the phone or on the Internet.

It does not apply to goods bought privately – in this case the seller must only describe the goods correctly and not mislead you.

### WHEN BUYING A SERVICE ...

Under the Supply of Goods and Services Act a service must be provided:

- **with reasonable care and skill** – the job should be done to a proper standard of workmanship.

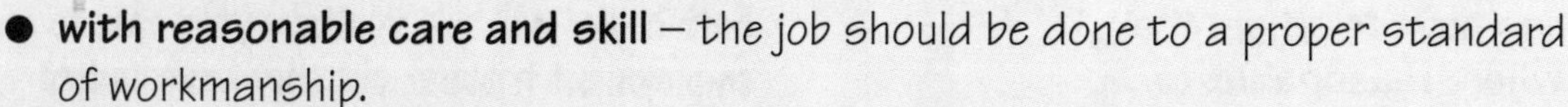

- **within a reasonable time** – even if you haven't agreed a definite completion date with the supplier of the service.
- **for a reasonable charge** – unless you agreed a price beforehand (NB an estimate tells you roughly what the cost will be. A quotation tells you the exact price – it is part of the contract between you and the supplier.)

'Reasonable' means compared with the normal standard that applies, e.g. what you would normally expect from a plumber/hairdresser, etc.

The Sale of Goods Act and the Supply of Goods and Services Act are civil laws. There are also some criminal laws that protect the consumer.

- The Trades Description Act: it is illegal to make a false description about goods or services.
- The Consumer Protection Act: it is illegal to sell unsafe goods or to mislead consumers about the price of goods. The manufacturer or importer is liable for any loss or damage caused.
- The Food Safety Act: it is illegal to sell food that doesn't comply with food safety requirements.

## THE CONTRACT

*When you buy something, you and the seller make a deal, called a contract. A contract can be spoken or written, and it is legally binding in civil law* p.14➤.

- *Under the contract, the consumer offers to buy the goods and promises to pay the agreed price; the seller accepts the offer and agrees to supply the goods.*
- *The contract is with the seller, not the manufacturer. This means that if the buyer has a complaint it is the seller who has to sort things out.*
- *Under the contract, if there is nothing wrong with the goods, the buyer has no right to take them back. Some shops may choose to exchange goods or give refunds, but they don't have to do this.*

## HOW TO MAKE A COMPLAINT

**1.** Take the faulty item back to the shop as soon as possible and ask, firmly but politely, for a refund or for it to be exchanged.

If you are complaining about a service, give the supplier a chance to put the matter right.

*Are you satisfied now?*

**2.** Write a firm but polite letter explaining your complaint to the customer services manager or company chairman/woman. Describe what action you've taken and what you want the firm to do.

*Are you satisfied now?*

**3.** Write a letter warning the seller or supplier that you will take legal action unless they act by a certain date.

*Are you satisfied now?*

**4.** Take your case to one of the organisations that offer help and advice on consumer matters:

- your Citizens' Advice Bureau, consumer advice centre or law centre
- the local trading standards officer (**www.tradingstandards.gov.uk**)
- the trading association to which the supplier belongs.

**Key Words**

civil law • consumer • contract • criminal law • responsibility •

## ACTIVITIES

1. **Working with a partner, discuss or invent (a) one purchase which contravenes the Sale of Goods Act, and (b) one service which contravenes the Supply of Goods and Services Act. Be prepared to justify your choice to the class.**
2. **Give an example of goods that you or your family have recently exchanged or had refunded. Why did this happen? Why do you think the shop was willing to agree to this exchange or refund?**
3. **In pairs, role-play two situations: (a) you are returning a faulty item to a shop to get a refund, (b) you want to change a CD as you made the wrong choice first time.**
4. **Look at the situations on Worksheet 32.**

# CHANGING SOCIETY

**This lesson considers three ways in which people can alter society for the better. Trade unions have been hugely important in changing society to recognise the rights of employees. We have the opportunity to work for our society in more ways than earning a living: volunteering is a growing factor in democratic life. As responsible consumers we can consider the social and ethical implications of our purchases.**

## TRADE UNIONS

### WHAT ARE TRADE UNIONS FOR?

**A trade union is an association of workers in a particular trade or profession, who join together to promote their interests by:**

- **protecting their jobs**
- **negotiating with employers (collective bargaining) on such issues as pay levels and working conditions**
- **offering help and services to members on legal and financial matters and training, etc.**

### A SHORT HISTORY OF TRADE UNIONS

**1834** The Tolpuddle Martyrs – six farm labourers who try to form a union to increase their wages are sentenced to seven years' transportation to Australia.

**1860s** Pay and conditions in Victorian Britain are appalling. Skilled workers are eventually allowed to join trade unions, which bargain for a better deal.

**1868** The Trades Union Congress (TUC), the national body of trade unions, is formed.

**1880s** With the development of industrialisation, semi-skilled and unskilled workers join unions p.57.

**1900** The TUC helps to form the Labour Party; gradually, employment laws are passed to protect workers. The trade unions maintain a strong link with the Labour Party until the 1990s p.29.

**1936** The General Strike: key industries in the transport and power industries strike in support of the mineworkers.

**1980s** Laws are passed to restrict union power and activities after a wave of strikes. Union membership falls with decline of heavy industry, and there is an increase in part-time jobs and a loosening of labour laws.

**1990s** Unions modernise to change their image and make services more relevant to their members. Many merge to gain greater bargaining power.

### TYPES OF UNION

| Type | Members | Example |
|---|---|---|
| **1** General unions | Large memberships from a range of industries | UNISON (for public and private sector employees) |
| **2** Craft unions | Skilled craftspeople with a particular skill | Musicians' Union |
| **3** Industrial unions | Workers in a particular industry | National Union of Mineworkers |
| **4** White-collar unions | Workers in non-manual occupations | National Union of Teachers |

# VOLUNTARY WORK

Volunteers play a huge role in providing public services in the UK. Twenty-two million adults each year do some sort of voluntary work, including:

- 30 000 magistrates, who deal with most criminal cases in England
- 12 700 special constables who help the police
- lifeboat personnel, and Red Cross and St John's Ambulance volunteers who provide first aid at public events
- 170 000 volunteers in the NHS and 100 000 in social care.

There are benefits of volunteering for both the individual and the community:

- For the individual – self-esteem, increased civic responsibility, greater social activity, learning new skills and taking on new challenges p.5➤.
- For the community – improved services, cleaner environment, a strengthened community based on empowering people, strengthening the bonds between them and a belief that individuals can influence society.

Community Service Volunteers (CSV) is a charity which creates opportunities for people to volunteer and make a difference to their communities. It campaigns for all public bodies to produce a citizen involvement policy which would explore ways in which communities and individuals can get involved.

There are opportunities for voluntary work abroad pp.91, 81➤.

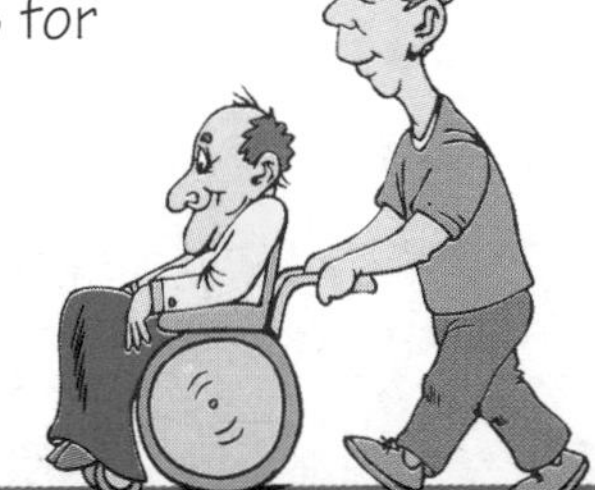

# CONSUMER CHOICE = CONSUMER POWER

***If enough people buy or refuse to buy a certain product, that will affect its price and availability. In this way consumers can use their power to influence what goods are available and how expensive they are*** p.60➤.

***Consumer responsibility means to take into account the social and ethical factors that go into producing or selling the goods. In recent years consumers have influenced products in many such areas, including:***

- ***environmentally friendly goods – by not buying aerosols which damage the ozone layer, and buying goods made from recycled materials*** p.90➤
- ***healthy food – by increasing purchase of, for example, vegetarian food and organic food, both of which also impact on our use of animals and the environment***
- ***cruelty-free goods – by not buying cosmetics, toiletries and household products that have been tested on animals; by not buying fur and other products made from dead animals***
- ***fair trade goods – which ensure that the people who produce the raw materials benefit more.***

**Key Words**

consumer • responsibility
right • trade union

## ACTIVITIES

1. **Write down three ways in which trade unions help their members.**
2. **Compile a survey of trade unions by using the questionnaire on Worksheet 33. When you have finished, combine your results with others in your group and create a wall display to show what you have learned.**
3. **In groups, discuss whether there are any products that you do not buy because of your beliefs.**
4. **Investigate the work of Community Service Volunteers through their website www.csv.org.uk. Write down three advantages and three disadvantages of voluntary work.**

# THE GROWTH OF THE EU

**The European Union (EU) is now a hugely important part of British life, influencing areas such as the economy, environment, legal system and the very idea of democracy and citizenship. To understand why this is the case, we need to look at the historical context.**

## A SHORT HISTORY OF EUROPE

*European history is a history of conflict between states.*

| | |
|---|---|
| 55 BC | Julius Caesar invades Britain (Italy v. Britain) |
| 1066 AD | Norman Conquest (France v. England) |
| 1337–1453 | Hundred Years' War (England v. France) |
| 1517 | The Reformation divides the Christian Church (Protestants v. Catholics) |
| 1588 | Spanish Armada (Spain v. England) |
| 1618–1648 | Thirty Years' War (Germany, France, Spain, Sweden) |
| 1756–1763 | Seven Years' War (Prussia, Britain, Spain v. Russia, France, Austria) |
| 1803–1815 | Napoleonic Wars (France v. rest of Europe) |
| 1870–1871 | Franco-Prussian War (France v. Prussia) |
| 1914–1918 | First World War (Germany, Turkey v. France, Britain, Italy, Russia, USA) |
| 1939–1945 | Second World War (Germany, Italy, Japan v. Britain, France, Russia, USA) |
| 1945–1989 | Cold War (Eastern Europe v. Western Europe) |

## THE PURPOSE OF THE EU

*By the middle of the twentieth century, Europe had already been devastated by two terrible world wars. In particular, France and Germany had been at war with each other three times in 80 years.*

*After the Second World War, therefore, France and Germany decided that they should work together with other European states in two ways.*

**POLITICALLY** – *To ensure peace by preventing Germany or any other power from dominating the other countries.*

**ECONOMICALLY** – *To bring economic strength and prosperity to Europe.*

### NEW FORMS OF POLITICAL CO-OPERATION

1. EU members at first chose to work together as individual nation states, with responsibilities mainly in agriculture, environment, trade and regional policies. This form of co-operation is called intergovernmentalism.
2. In the last decade, however, the EU has become more federalist. In a federal organisation the nation states give up some of their powers to a central government p.23. European integration means strengthening European institutions in this federalist manner p.76.

### NEW FORMS OF ECONOMIC CO-OPERATION

1. The single market (or common market) is one in which there are no trade barriers between member states. This means abolishing tariffs (taxes) charged on goods bought from other member countries, and allowing free movement of goods, money and people across frontiers.
2. The single currency (or monetary union), under the control of a Central European Bank, means abolishing exchange rates between member countries, and that only one currency (the euro) is used by all p.80.

## STEPPING STONES TO EUROPEAN INTEGRATION

1951 Treaty of Paris. The European Coal and Steel Community is set up by 'The Six' (France, Germany, Italy, Belgium, Netherlands, Luxembourg).

1957 Treaty of Rome. The Six set up the European Economic Community (EEC).

1973 The UK, Ireland and Denmark join the EEC. Norwegians vote not to join.

1979 First direct elections to the European Parliament are held.

1981 Greece joins the EEC.

1986 Spain and Portugal join the EEC.

1992 The Maastricht Treaty creates the European Union (EU) and presents a blueprint for closer economic and political union.

1993 The single market is launched.

1995 Austria, Finland and Sweden join the EU – Norway again says no.

1999 The single currency – the euro – is launched.

## EU MEMBER STATES 2003

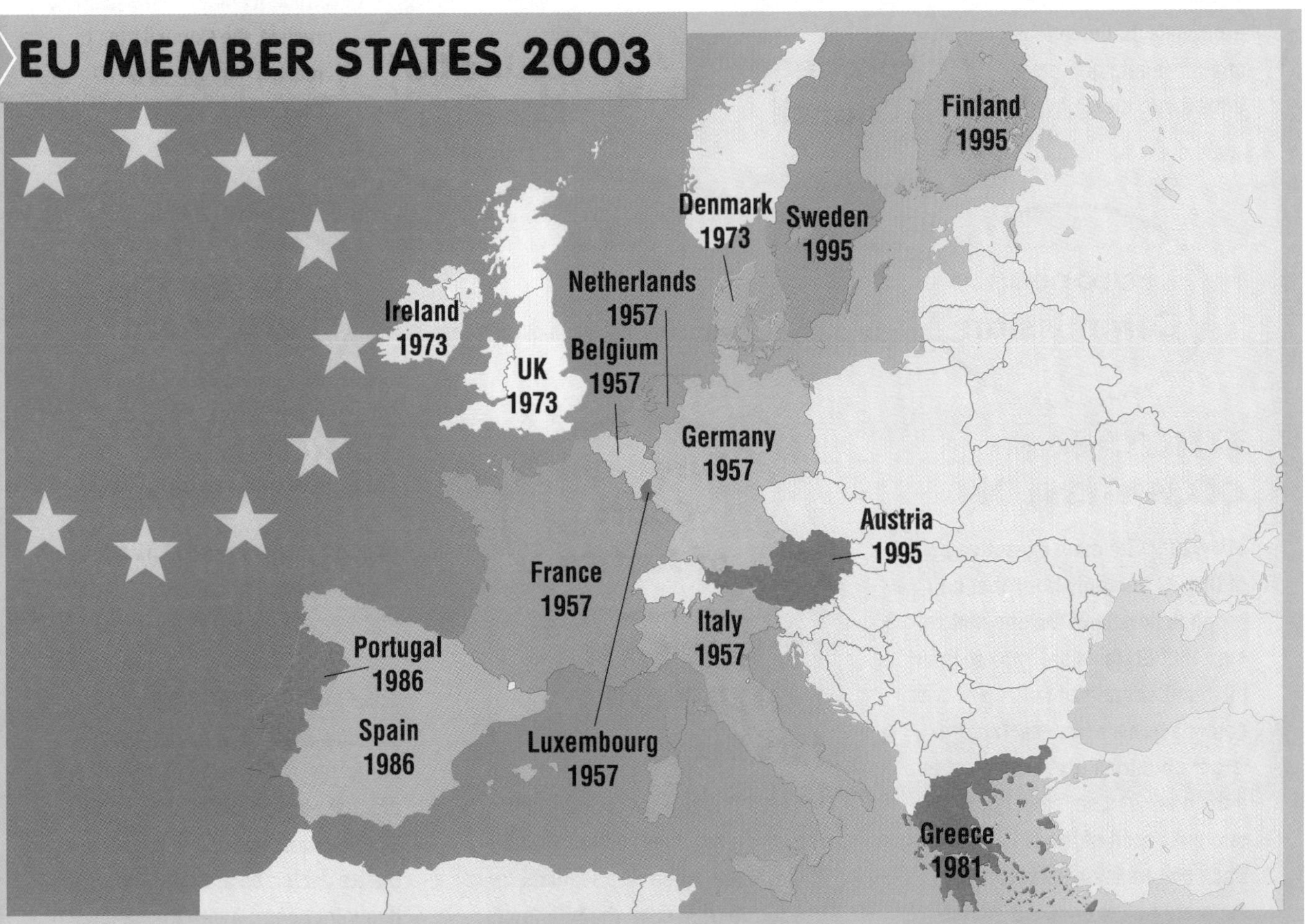


## ACTIVITIES

1. Write down the two main reasons why the European Union was formed.
2. Describe in your own words what is meant by:
   (a) nation state, (b) European integration,
   (c) single market, (d) single currency.
3. Do you think the EU has succeeded in its main aims?
4. Complete the 'Finding out about the EU', questions on Worksheet 34.

**Key Words**

European integration
federalism • intergovernmentalism
single currency • single market

# SPOTLIGHT ON THE EU

The EU is a huge and complex organisation with five main institutions, each one of which has representatives from the 15 member states.

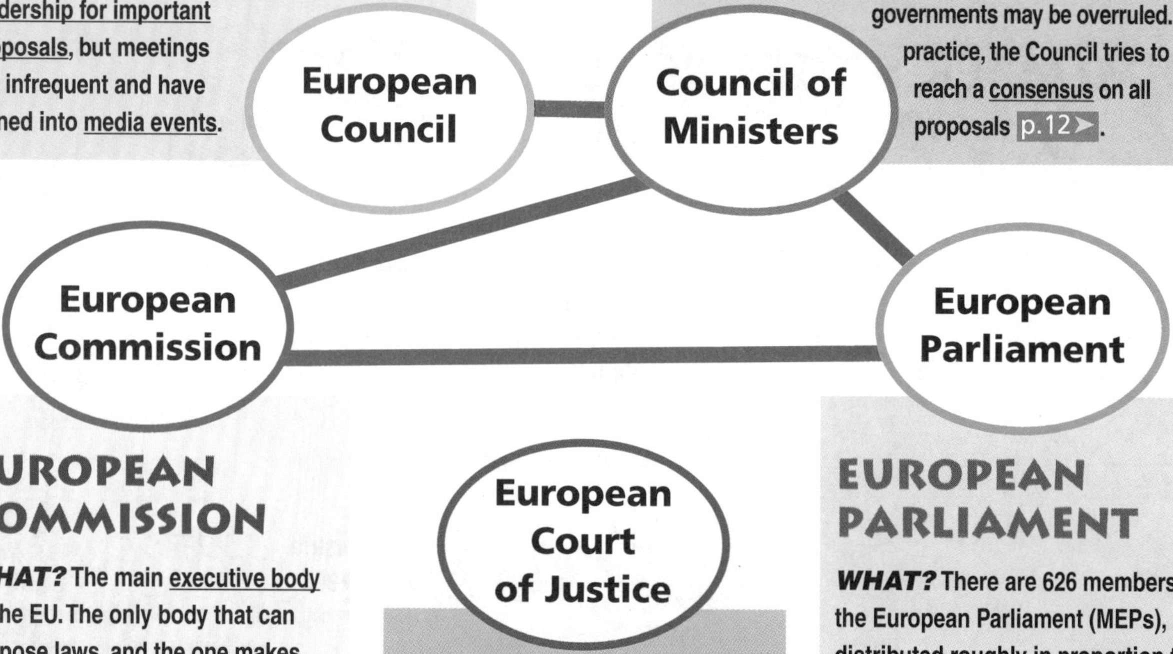

## EUROPEAN COUNCIL

***WHAT?*** This consists of the heads of government plus foreign ministers. They meet at least twice a year to take important decisions that can only be made at this high political level.
***WHERE?*** In different capital cities, depending on which country holds the presidency.
***DEMOCRACY CHECK*** ☒ A different country holds the presidency every six months. The European Council provides leadership for important proposals, but meetings are infrequent and have turned into media events.

## COUNCIL OF MINISTERS

***WHAT?*** The main legislative and decision-making body of the EU, which meets nearly 100 times a year. Made up of one member from each state (the choice of minister depending on the subject being discussed) along with the relevant commissioners.
***WHERE?*** Brussels
***DEMOCRACY CHECK*** ☒ The bigger the country, the more votes it has. Majority voting is used for most decisions, which means that individual governments may be overruled. In practice, the Council tries to reach a consensus on all proposals p.12 ➤.

European Council — Council of Ministers — European Commission — European Parliament — European Court of Justice

## EUROPEAN COMMISSION

***WHAT?*** The main executive body of the EU. The only body that can propose laws, and the one makes sure that EU laws are implemented by member states. Made up of two commissioners from each of the larger countries (to be reduced to one commissioner from 2005) and one from each of the smaller states. Each commissioner oversees a separate policy area, e.g. transport. There are 20 000 permanent staff.
***WHERE?*** Brussels.
***DEMOCRACY CHECK*** ☒
Commissioners are appointed, not elected. They are not meant to represent their countries but to act independently to serve the general interest. Allegations of mismanagement and sleaze in the late 1990s have led to proposals for reform.

## EUROPEAN COURT OF JUSTICE

***WHAT?*** The highest court in the EU, which resolves disputes about EU laws and treaties. It is made up of one judge from each member state.
***WHERE?*** Luxembourg.
***DEMOCRACY CHECK*** ☒
The rule of law is a vital pillar of democracy. Any citizen of the EU can bring a case to the Court, which has the power to overturn decisions made in the citizen's own country. As European law takes precedence over the law of each member state, this is effectively a lessening of national sovereignty.

## EUROPEAN PARLIAMENT

***WHAT?*** There are 626 members of the European Parliament (MEPs), distributed roughly in proportion to the size of the country's population. Their main job is to supervise the Commission and the Council of Ministers. The European Parliament discusses proposals made by the Commission and can amend them, but its decisions are not binding. It has joint control (with the Council of Ministers) over the EU budget.
***WHERE?*** Parliament: Strasbourg. Its committees: Brussels.
***DEMOCRACY CHECK*** ☒
Meetings are open to the public, and voting is by simple majority. It is the only body directly elected by citizens of the EU (once every five years), but it is also the least powerful of the five key institutions p.80 ➤.

# SPOTLIGHT ON THE EU

**How is the EU run? How democratic is it?**



## THE BUDGET

### INCOME

The EU receives contributions from its member states according to their ability to pay. The richer countries, such as the UK and Germany, are called net contributors because they pay out more than they receive; they effectively subsidise the poorer countries. Income also comes from a share of Value Added Tax (VAT) raised in the member states, and from customs duties.

**EU income, 2000**

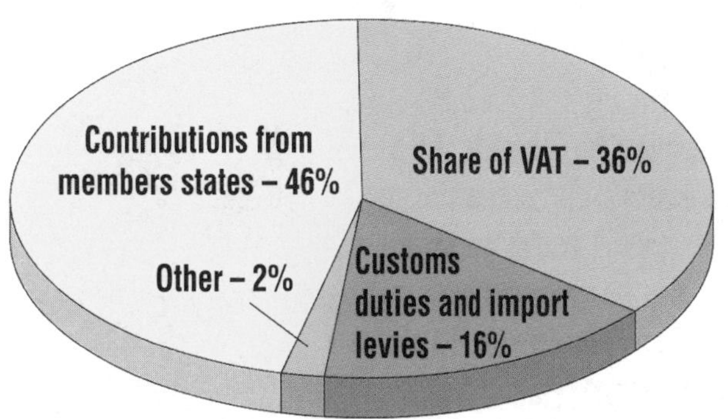


### EXPENDITURE

The largest two items of EU expenditure are subsidies for farmers (the Common Agricultural Policy, or CAP) and funds for regional policies which aid development across the EU.

The Common Agricultural Policy was introduced in 1962 as a means of getting states to co-operate in food production. It subsidised farmers by setting artificially high prices for agricultural products, and it bought up goods to keep prices stable.

However, the policy:

- encouraged farmers to be inefficient
- allowed huge surpluses to build up
- encouraged intensive farming methods
- led to British food prices rising, as British farms were already competitive.

Reforms to CAP in the 1980s and 1990s have aimed to reduce the level of price support and limit the amount that farmers produce. But inefficiencies still remain, and CAP is one of the most controversial of all EU policies.

**EU expenditure, 2000**

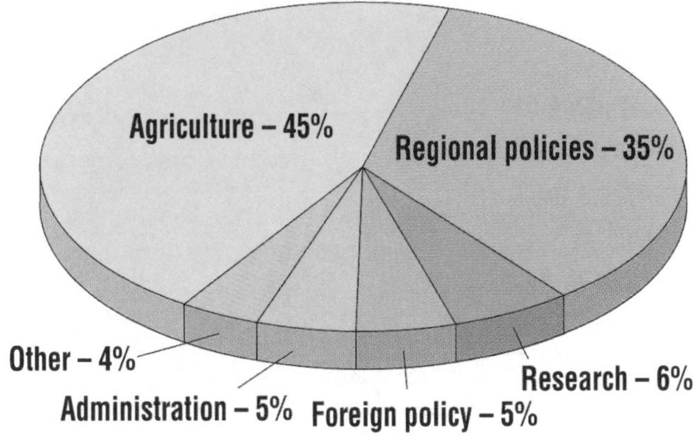


### ACTIVITIES

1. Compare the EU system of government with the UK's. What are the similarities and differences?
2. How democratic is the EU? Worksheet 35 focuses on the European Parliament.
3. Why do you think most of the EU's budget goes towards subsidising farmers and poorer regions of the member states? Is this fair?

**Key Words**

democracy • executive • legislature
rule of law • sovereignty

# CITIZENS OF EUROPE

- **Every citizen of an EU member state is also a citizen of the EU. How does being a citizen of the EU affect you?**
- **These pages show ten of the most important effects that the EU has on our daily life in Britain.**

## 1 TRAVEL

You have the right to move and live anywhere within the EU. All citizens have a European passport, which makes it easier to cross borders and go through customs. An E111 form allows you to claim a refund for any medical treatment that you have paid for while in an EU country pp. 82–83.

## 2 EDUCATION AND EMPLOYMENT

The EU runs educational and training programmes to encourage study, work experience and exchanges between member states. Qualifications are recognised in other EU states. The Social Chapter of the Maastricht Treaty aims to improve conditions of employment via a range of regulations, including working hours and pay, and health and safety issues pp.62–63.

## 3 CONSUMER AFFAIRS

Tight rules to create common product standards are in place in shops and industries across the EU. This harmonisation protects our health and safety, as well as enabling the single market to be truly a 'common' market.

## 4 HUMAN RIGHTS

The EU campaigns against racism and discrimination in all its forms, both in EU countries and in the wider world. The European Convention on Human Rights has now been incorporated into British law (in the Human Rights Act 1998): all our laws must conform to the rights listed under the Convention pp. 8–9.

## 5 DEMOCRATIC RIGHTS AND POWERS

All citizens have the right to vote and stand in the European and local elections (but not the national elections) of other member states. However, the main centre of power in Britain's democracy has moved significantly away from Parliament, as EU institutions are now the most important decision-making bodies p. 77.

## 6 ENVIRONMENT

The EU has enacted over 200 measures to 'preserve, protect and improve the quality of the environment'. These cover areas such as air and noise pollution, bathing beaches, drinking water, forests, wildlife and waste disposal. Big building projects must now take into account their environmental impact. There is an EU eco-label for environmentally-friendly products p.89.

## 7 STANDARD OF LIVING

A major aim of the EU's single market is to improve the economic performance of the region as a whole, so that everyone's standard of living is raised. The European Regional Development Fund provides help for poorer regions of the EU, including declining industrial and rural areas in Britain, by developing their infrastructure p.73.

## 8 ECONOMY

Joining the EU has had several major effects on the British economy:

- economic policy-making has been Europeanised – important decisions are now made in Brussels, not London
- the UK now does far more trade with EU states than it did 25 years ago
- Britain's highly free market economy has been moderated by the more regulated, state-controlled European economic model p.55.

## 9 LAW AND LEGAL RIGHTS

European law now covers much of our life, especially in the areas of business, agriculture, the environment, discrimination and civil liberties. European regulations automatically become law in Britain; European directives indicate what the law should be, allowing Parliament to pass its own laws to that effect. EU law has precedence over UK law p.12.

## 10 CULTURE AND THE ARTS

Each year the EU gives grants to a different 'cultural capital of Europe' to develop its cultural and artistic life. In addition, several 'European Cities of Culture' are chosen each year.

## ACTIVITIES

1. List the *three* aspects of daily life and public affairs that you think are the *most* affected by Britain's membership of the EU. Share your list in small groups – do you agree?
2. Write one paragraph describing the benefits of being a citizen of the European Union.
3. Decide how British you feel (on scale of 1 to 10), and how European you feel. Discuss the results in groups. Do you think you would say the same (a) 50 years ago, (b) in 50 years' time?
4. Read the account of the kidnapped UK business man on Worksheet 36 and answer the questions. Contact Amnesty International for more information about political prisoners.

# FLASHPOINT EUROPE

**Many aspects of the EU – and of Britain's attitude to the EU – are controversial.**

## SEMI-DETACHED BRITAIN

FLASHPOINT

***Britain has been described as a 'semi-detached' member of the EU, as it has*** *never been enthusiastic about European integration. There are several reasons suggested for this:*

- *National pride – Some believe Britain is hanging on to 'great power' status after victory in the Second World War*
- *Others say that Britain's island mentality, stemming from its* ***geographical position on the edge of Europe, stops it being a true partner***
- *It is said it has too many trade and cultural links with non-European countries (the Commonwealth, USA), especially English-speaking countries* p.78
- *Some blame Britain's distinctive form of parliamentary government*
- *Others blame its highly free market economy, which is closer to the US model than to the European model* p.55.

## CLOSER EUROPEAN UNION?

FLASHPOINT

The European question dominates British politics: should Britain support a strengthening of the EU or remain semi-detached and on the sidelines?

| The case FOR closer union | | The case AGAINST closer union |
|---|---|---|
| A single currency and other economic and financial measures will make the EU more competitive and prosperous in the world economy. | **Economy** | A single currency is too inflexible and could lead to economic difficulties in certain regions. |
| Germany is still the dominant economic power in Europe – it needs to be locked in to closer union with the rest of Europe. | **Politics** | Closer union would lead to a 'United States of Europe' and greater loss of sovereignty. |
| The democracy of the EU needs to be improved, which means strengthening the institutions and making them more accountable to the people of Europe. | **Democracy** | The EU's institutions are not democratic enough, and the EU is too large and too distant ever to be properly democratic. |
| The EU should have a common foreign and defence policy to meet the challenges of an unstable world. | **Security** | A common foreign and defence policy will be difficult to achieve, ineffective and an unwelcome step towards a European superstate. |
| Britain's opt-out on the single currency and other matters weakens the Union as a whole and encourages disintegration. | **The opt-out** | Britain's pragmatic approach allows it to respond more flexibly to economic and political conditions, and to look after its own interests. |

The three main political parties in Britain have different attitudes to closer European union. The Conservative Party is the least enthusiastic about closer European union. The Labour Party supports closer union if there are clear benefits for Britain. The Liberal Democrats are in favour of greater European integration in principle p.29.

# AN EROSION OF SOVEREIGNTY? FLASHPOINT

Sovereignty means having complete control over your own affairs. The EU impacts on the national sovereignty of its member states.

- Eurosceptics wish to resist further transfer of powers from national parliaments to EU institutions. They are concerned about the erosion of sovereignty that is the inevitable result of closer political and economic union. They want states to run their affairs as independently as possible.
- Pro-Europeans see this loss of sovereignty as a price worth paying for being part of a larger, successful and peaceful European superpower. They also view federalism in a more positive light, not so much as a centralised form of government as a loosely organised one in which member states have the right to run many of their own affairs. These rights are supported by the principle of subsidiarity (see box, right).

According to the principle of subsidiarity, decisions should be taken at national, regional or even local level within each country, except where they have to be taken at European level. However, the principle is not backed up by law.

# ENLARGEMENT FLASHPOINT

Membership is open to any European state that respects 'the principles of liberty, democracy, respect for human rights and fundamental freedoms, and the rule of law'. To date, 13 more countries from Central and Eastern Europe have applied to join the EU, including former communist countries. Although all existing members accept the principle of enlargement, there are advantages and disadvantages:

**FOR:**

1. greater democracy and security within Europe
2. a larger market in which to trade
3. a stronger Europe in the world.

**AGAINST:**

1. difficulty reaching an agreement between so many countries
2. huge increase in bureaucracy
3. EU institutions will need to be reformed to cope with the numbers.

Whether the EU institutions should be strengthened or diluted to cope with enlargement depends on whether you have a more federal or intergovernmental approach to Europe p.70.

## Key Words

European integration • federalism • free market economy • intergovernmentalism • sovereignty • subsidiarity

## ACTIVITIES

1. Write one paragraph explaining why Britain's attitude towards Europe is often described as 'semi-detached'.
2. Explain what the following terms mean: (a) national sovereignty, (b) federalism, (c) subsidiarity, (d) Eurosceptics.
3. Hold a class debate with the motion: 'This house believes that closer European union is good for Britain and for Europe.' Use the information on Worksheet 37 to help you with this.
4. In groups, discuss what you think will be the effect on the EU of enlargement from 15 members to double that number. Then write a statement of your own attitude to this.

# THE UK AND THE WORLD

**What of Britain's relations with the wider world? The last 50 years has been a period of intense globalisation and interdependency pp.82–83. Institutions have developed so that nation states can co-operate with each other. The seeds of this process were sown in six extraordinary years after the end of the Second World War.**

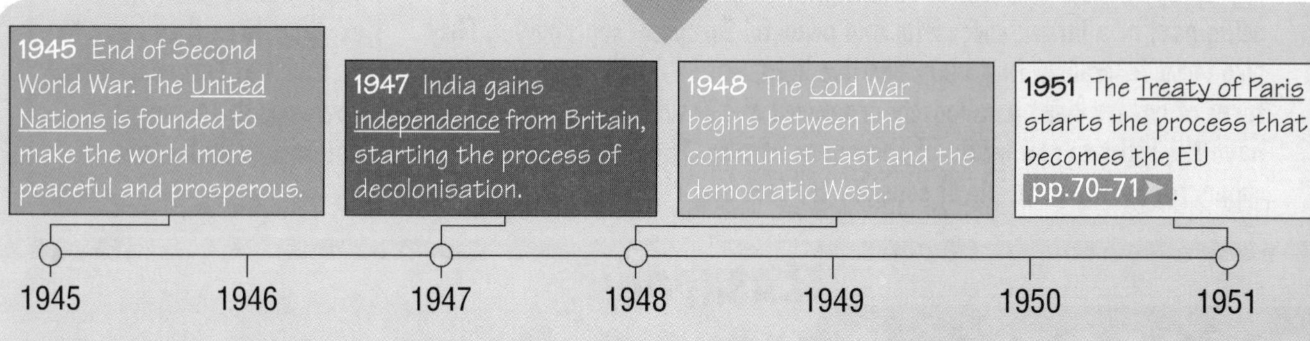


## THE COMMONWEALTH

Decolonisation was the process by which British colonies such as India and Kenya gained their independence. To maintain links between these ex-colonies, however, the Commonwealth was created. The Commonwealth is now a voluntary association of countries across the world, from Canada to Australia, headed by the British sovereign.

- The Commonwealth meets to discuss trade, development and international issues; it is not a great power on the world stage.
- As their former ruler, Britain has an uneasy relationship with some Commonwealth countries.
- Britain looks more towards the USA and Europe than Commonwealth countries as trading and political partners.

## NATO

In 1949, feeling threatened by the Soviet Union, Britain joined with the USA and ten other countries in western Europe and North America to set up a political and military alliance – the North Atlantic Treaty Organisation (NATO). With the end of the Cold War and the collapse of the Soviet Union (1991), NATO's main aim has since been to promote peace and democracy throughout Europe and North America.

- NATO now has 19 members, some of which are former Communist countries, such as Poland.
- A new NATO-Russia Council gives Russia partial membership of NATO.
- NATO has adopted a primarily peacekeeping role, for example in the war in Bosnia (1992–5).

There is some criticism of NATO, however.

- Some people have questioned whether a military organisation is necessary now that the Cold War is over.
- NATO's war against Serbia over ethnic cleansing in Kosovo (1999) was controversial; it did not have the approval of the UN Security Council.
- NATO has been seen as a means for the USA to interfere in Europe's affairs.

# THE UNITED NATIONS

Britain was one of the 51 countries that set up the United Nations in New York in 1945. They agreed to work together to create a world free from war and to bring justice and equality. There are now 189 members of the UN, each of which has one vote in the General Assembly. They pay for the cost of the organisation in proportion to their wealth. The UN has several roles:

- **Peace and security**, handled by the Security Council, which has 15 members. The five permanent members are China, USA, UK, France and Russia. The Security Council decides how to intervene in disputes, whether through sanctions, negotiation, peacekeeping or military force.
- **Justice and human rights.** The UN Commission on Human Rights upholds the Universal declaration of Human Rights and deals with human rights abuses in the world p.8. The International Court of Justice at The Hague, the Netherlands, is the world's court, which rules on questions of international law.
- **Social and economic development.** A large proportion of UN work is aimed at improving the standard of living of the world's poor. It does this through specialised agencies such as the World Health Organisation (WHO), the World Bank, the Food and Agriculture Organisation (FAO) and the International Children's Emergency Fund (UNICEF) p.87.

Most people think that the UN has been very successful in creating a better world through its humanitarian and social programmes. Its peacekeeping efforts have been far less effective, for two main reasons:

1 the lack of military muscle and authority behind the UN forces
2 the individual interests of the permanent members of the Security Council, who can stop any decision they don't like.

## ACTIVITIES

**Key Words**
decolonisation • globalisation
interdependency

1. **In groups, discuss what the Commonwealth is, and whether it has an important role to play in the world. In pairs or as individuals, find out more about the Commonwealth using the first part of Worksheet 38.**
2. **Write a paragraph explaining the aims of the United Nations. Add a personal view on whether it has succeeded in its aims. Use the second part of Worksheet 38 to help you with this.**
3. **Use the Internet and your library to compile a factsheet on NATO.**

# CHANGING SOCIETY

**The European and international organisations that have been the focus of this unit may appear to be huge and distant institutions over which ordinary citizens have little power or influence. Yet there are opportunities for individuals and groups to bring about changes, even at this level.**

## A REFERENDUM ON THE EURO

When an important decision must be taken on a single issue, governments can ask the people to decide by voting in a referendum p.33➤. The Labour government has promised a referendum on the issue of whether to join Economic and Monetary Union (EMU) p.70➤. Twelve member states have already joined, which means that the euro replaces their national currencies, and that monetary and economic policy is centrally controlled by a European Central Bank. What arguments will persuade British citizens to vote yes or no?

The euro is the future. It means you won't have to change currency when you travel through Europe. It makes business transactions and planning easier as exchange rates will be fixed.

Price differences between the same goods across Europe will be clearer. I want to be at the centre of Europe, not on the edge!

I don't want to lose the pound. It would be a sign of our loss of control over our financial affairs.

Interest rates could go up when Britain needs them to go down.

It will also lead to EU control of our taxes – full political union will be next! Besides, Britain's economy is strong enough to stand on its own.

## CONTROLLING THE EU

1. **The European Parliament is the only directly elected parliament of any international organisation. Although many people think that it still has too little power compared with the Council of Ministers, elections to the European Parliament, held every five years, are an opportunity for individuals to have their say. The UK elects 87 Members of the European Parliament (MEPs) by proportional representation** p.72➤.
2. **There are over 500 pressure groups currently lobbying EU institutions. This is an essential means of persuading the EU to conduct its policy along lines acceptable to your own special interest, whether that is farming or the protection of birds** p.32➤.
3. **Regional and local authorities in Britain have a European office to make effective contact with the EU and to receive aid from the EU's funds. The links between local and regional bodies and the EU are increasing, building alliances which often bypass national government at Westminster. This is an example of the decentralising tendency of a federal institution** pp.30–31➤.

# HELPING THE UNITED NATIONS

The United Nations Volunteer programme (UNV) is the volunteer arm of the UN. Each year about 5000 qualified and experienced men and women of over 150 nationalities volunteer their services in developing and war-torn countries across the world. These UN volunteers:

- provide humanitarian assistance, such as protecting children and refugees, and monitoring food aid
- assist in peacekeeping missions and help to monitor elections
- promote longer-term reconstruction and development initiatives.

UNV is one way in which individuals can contribute to an interdependent society by building trust and reciprocity between citizens.

# CAMPAIGNING AGAINST ARMS

There are many pressure groups which have an international dimension. These are open to any individual who wishes to help them in their work of persuading governments and international organisations to change their policies p.32➤.

The Campaign Against the Arms Trade (CAAT) was set up in the UK in 1974 by a number of organisations that were concerned about the growth in the arms trade. Developing countries spend over $2 billion a year on arms, but nearly all the weapons traded are supplied by only six countries, one of which is Britain. CAAT works to end the international arms trade as it believes that arms exports:

- encourage wars, most of which have been fought with imported arms
- waste valuable resources, which could be used to reduce poverty and disease
- support repressive regimes, such as that of Indonesia, which Britain supplied with arms and jets despite knowing that it would use them against its own people.

**Key Words**
decentralisation • referendum • volunteer

## ACTIVITIES

1. Investigate the different views on the issue of Britain joining the euro by logging on to www.ukonline.gov.uk and clicking on 'newsroom' and 'hot topics'. Then write a statement saying whether you would vote for or against joining the euro in a referendum.
2. Discuss whether you feel you have any control over the policies of the EU.
3. How can you make an impact on the international scene? Discuss this question in groups, then write a paragraph giving your own views.
4. Discuss in class the 'No bombing' leaflet shown on Worksheet 39.

# KEY TRENDS IN GLOBALISATION

## GLOBAL CAPITALISM

- Free market capitalism has become the dominant economic system in the world, especially after the fall of communism. The World Trade Organisation, which sets the rules for world trade on free trade lines, has 144 member countries pp.55, 86.
- Governments have moved towards deregulation, privatisation and cutting back on state expenditure. Workforces have had to become more flexible, with more part-time contracts, multiskilling and less power for the unions p.68.

## GLOBAL POLITICS

- Governments increasingly work together to solve problems, forming international organisations such as the EU, UN and NATO. This process has increased since the end of the Cold War in 1989, which had split the world into two opposing camps pp.78–79.
- Groups of nations pool their political power at the expense of national governments, e.g. the EU pp.70–77 and the Association of South East Asian Nations (ASEAN).

## GLOBAL TECHNOLOGY

- Rapid growth in information and communication technologies (ICT), especially the Internet has made the world seem smaller by speeding up communication and establishing a new 'information economy' pp.52–53.
- Better transport has allowed freer and quicker movement of goods.

## GLOBAL MEDIA AND CULTURE

- Multimedia giants such as News International produce and market products for world consumption p.51.
- Digital and satellite TV means that countries across the world watch similar programmes.
- Traditional values and cultures are increasingly open to global consumer products such as MacDonald's hamburgers and Nike trainers.

## GLOBAL ECONOMY

- The world's economy has become more integrated. Money and goods flow across national boundaries as never before (see diagram below).
- There are over 50 000 transnational corporations (TNCs), which are huge businesses operating from more than one country. They account for a third of world trade, and their decisions are often more important than the decisions of governments.

Industrialised countries → Developing countries:
- Export manufactured goods
- Provide foreign aid
- Provide technology and investment

Industrialised countries ⟷ **economic interdependence** ⟷ Developing countries

Developing countries → Industrialised countries:
- Export primary products and manufactured goods
- Repay debts
- Provide immigrant labour

# GLOBALISATION

**Globalisation describes how people, businesses and governments across the world are becoming more interdependent and interconnected. Globalisation has many features, and it is a controversial process.**

## IS GLOBALISATION GOOD FOR YOU?

Whether globalisation is good or bad for the world is a controversial question. Here are some of the arguments.

### ADVANTAGES

- Globalisation draws people closer together and shows that we are all citizens of one world.
- World trade has increased hugely over the last 50 years, bringing variety and choice to the consumer and greater prosperity through economic growth.
- TNCs lower production costs and provide cheaper goods and services for all. The foreign investment that they bring provides jobs and spreads technology and skills.
- The technological revolution has transformed work and leisure practices, making lives easier for millions in wealthier countries.
- International news services such as CNN and the BBC World Service provide an alternative source of news in countries that lack a democratic media.

### DISADVANTAGES

- Globalisation has increased the gap between rich and poor countries. Much of the foreign investment has gone to countries with stronger economies.
- TNCs mean lower wages and worse conditions for workers in poorer countries. TNCs are unaccountable and have too much power.
- Capitalism has become dominant, with its tendency to put profit before human need. This also has negative effects on social conditions and the environment.
- Increasing interdependence means that a crisis in one country, e.g. recession in the USA, has a large effect on the world economy.
- Transnational media outlets control how information is presented across the world.
- There is an 'Americanisation' of consumer products and culture worldwide.

### Key Words

capitalism • deregulation
free market economy • globalisation
privatisation • transnational corporation

### ACTIVITIES

1. Describe in three sentences in your own words what globalisation means.
2. Discuss in small groups the advantages and disadvantages of globalisation. What verdict do you come to? Present your case to the class.
3. With a partner, discuss the concept of global citizenship described on Worksheet 40. In groups, choose the three global issues from the list on Worksheet 40 that you consider to be the most important.

# RICH WORLD, POOR WORLD

**The world is divided into rich nations and poor nations. Poverty means not just lack of money, but lack of opportunities to enjoy the health, housing, education and living standards that those in wealthier nations take for granted.**

## CONTRASTS IN DEVELOPMENT

Development is the use of a country's natural resources and technology to improve its standard of living.

- The richer or more economically developed countries (MEDCs) are in the northern hemisphere (apart from Australia and New Zealand). MEDC countries are often called the North.
- The poorer or less economically developed countries (LEDCs) are in the southern hemisphere. LEDC countries are often called the South.

One measure of development is the United Nations' human development index (HDI), which takes into account a country's:

- economic development – its increase in income and wealth
- social development – improvements in health, education and the quality of life.

Measured by HDI, the countries of the world are very unequal in terms of their development (see below).

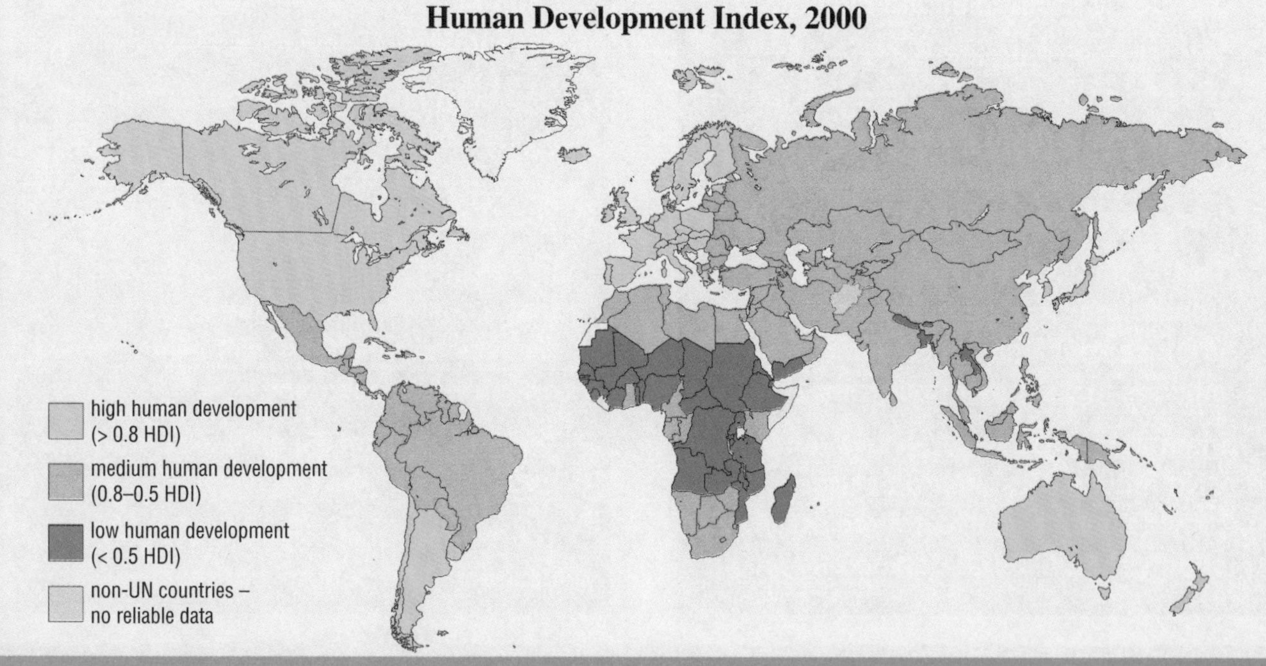


## RICH AND POOR

- *Half the world's population live on less than $2 per day.*
- *The top fifth of the world's people, who live in the highest income countries, have access to 85% of the world's wealth. The bottom fifth, in the poorest countries, has about 1%.*
- *The combined wealth of the world's three richest men is greater than that of the world's 48 poorest countries.*

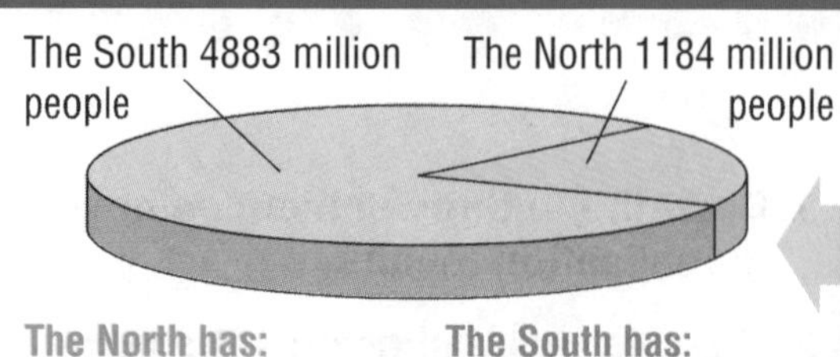


**The North has:**
20% world population
80% consumption of world's energy
85% of world's income

**The South has:**
80% world population
20% consumption of world's energy
15% of world's income

*World population, 2001*

# THE POVERTY TRAP

There are many factors which prevent a country from developing, and which contribute to poverty.

## HUNGER

- Lack of food results in tiredness, sickness, inability to work and death. Hungry people do not contribute to a country's economy.
- 840 million people per day in the South do not receive enough food.
- Poor countries cannot afford to change from growing cash crops (crops grown for export) to crops to feed their own people.

## TRADE AND DEBT

- Patterns of trade and debt prevent many countries from breaking the poverty cycle pp.86–87.

## EDUCATION

- Poor education contributes to poverty, as it leads to poorly paid jobs and unemployment.
- Poor families cannot afford to keep their children in school – they are needed to help the family by working.

## ENVIRONMENT

- Countries in the South are often located in areas prone to severe environmental conditions such as floods, droughts, earthquakes and storms.
- In such regions, deforestation, agribusiness and tourism damage the landscape and natural resources, thereby increasing poverty.
- Poorer countries have fewer resources to prevent and to deal with these problems, and the disasters drain their resources further.

## POPULATION

- Where population growth is faster than economic growth, there are more mouths to feed, more jobs to provide and greater pressure on the education and health resources of a country.
- The world's population is growing at the rate of 210 000 people every day: 98% of this growth is in Africa, Asia and South America.
- Women in Africa have an average of 6.5 children. In Europe the figure is 1.9 children.

## HEALTH

- Poor health and disease prevent people from escaping poverty, as incomes are lost and expenses go up.
- Malnutrition, poor housing and bad sanitation/water supply encourage diseases such as dysentery and pneumonia.
- HIV/AIDS is a major economic and social crisis for many poor countries. There were 3.8 million new cases in sub-Saharan Africa in 2000 and 5.8% of adults in Africa as a whole have AIDS.

## CONFLICT

- Wars devastate a country's economy as well as its people, and make the country less attractive for foreign investment.
- Conflict often occurs where there is a significant difference in wealth or human rights between sections of the community or region.
- Twenty of the world's 38 poorest countries are either fighting wars or just recovering from wars.

**Key Words**
development • LEDC • MEDC

## ACTIVITIES

1. **In groups of four, list what you think are the four greatest problems suffered by LEDCs, together with what you think is the best solution for each problem.**
2. **Worksheet 41 compares an MP from Ethiopia with an MP in the UK. In class, discuss the work of the two MPs. Individually, or in pairs, answer the question from the worksheet.**
3. **Find out about the global threat of AIDS (Worksheet 42), and the eight million people at risk of famine in Ethiopia (www.oxfam.org.uk/whatnew/press/ethiopia/.html).**

# TRADE AND AID

**There has been a huge expansion of world trade over the last few decades. This should have created greater prosperity, but the poorer countries have gained the least. As a result they borrow huge amounts of money from the richer countries; many countries in the South (LEDCs) also depend on aid from countries in the North (MEDCs).**

## AID

Many countries in the South depend on aid.

- Short-term aid is emergency aid which provides relief after a disaster. This aid consists of money, medicines, blankets, food, etc.
- Long-term aid aims to increase economic and social development, e.g. healthcare, education, improvements in the infrastructure.

### AID COMES FROM THREE MAIN SOURCES

#### 1. MULTILATERAL AID

This is aid given by international bodies such as the UN, World Bank and International Monetary Fund. These organisations promote long-term projects in health, agriculture and other areas. Critics say too many are prestige projects, such as power stations, dams and airports. Prestige projects:

- are very expensive to build and maintain, and can increase debt
- take little account of the needs of local people
- displace thousands of people and damage the environment.

#### 2. BILATERAL AID

This is aid given by one country direct to another. Much of Britain's aid budget is spent in this way. Critics say that this too has disadvantages.

- It is often given in the form of a loan, which increases debt.
- It is often tied aid, which means the money must be spent on goods sold by the donor country.

#### 3. NON-GOVERNMENTAL AID

Non-governmental organisations (NGOs) are charities such as Oxfam and Save the Children p.91 ➤.

- They are small but free from political bias, and more flexible than larger organisations and governments.
- They focus on small, long-term development projects aimed at the most needy. Many use appropriate (or intermediate) technology, which is cheaper, low-tech, sustainable and provides local employment.
- They emphasise self help among local people rather than imposing solutions from above.

## DEBT

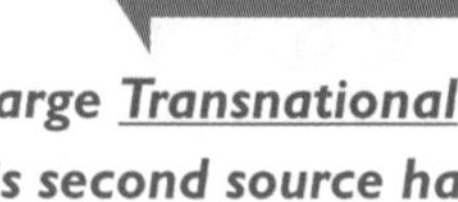

*LEDCs need money to invest in their economies. One source of investment is the large Transnational Corporations* pp.82–83 ➤*. Another is borrowing money from MEDCs. However, this second source has caused a huge problem of debt.*

- *Rises in interest rates in the 1980s and 1990s has meant that countries cannot even pay the interest on their loans, so they fall into greater debt.*
- *Many countries, especially in Africa, spend more on debt repayments than on health and education. The amount they owe is a high proportion of what they earn.*
- *Countries have got into debt partly because of bad management and corrupt regimes, and partly because of bad advice from MEDCs.*

# INTERNATIONAL TRADE

International trade has grown from $232 billion in 1960 to over $12 000 billion today. However, LEDCs benefit the least from world trade for several reasons.

- Many poorer countries export mainly primary products (food and raw materials). These are worth far less than the manufactured and processed goods exported by the richer industrialised countries.
- Poor countries also often depend on only a few cash crops, e.g. sugar or copper, which are subject to highly fluctuating prices on the international market.
- This pattern of trade is a direct result of 18th- and 19th-century colonialism, when European countries exploited their colonies to grow rich themselves. It is very hard for LEDCs to break out of this pattern of dependence.
- Although the World Trade Organisation, which has 144 member countries, is committed to free trade, there are still barriers to free trade which work against LEDCs, e.g. quotas (limits on the amount of processed goods imported) and subsidies to the home industries.

# TACKLING POVERTY AND DEBT

**All of the problems outlined in this and the last lesson can be tackled successfully.**

**Population.** Birth control programmes and family planning. Improving countries' economies reduces the need for large families.
**Education.** Investment in education is necessary to train a workforce short in skills and literacy.
**Conflict.** Promoting democracy and human rights leads to political stability and peace, so that resources can be targeted on development.
**Health.** Investment in healthcare, and especially providing safe water supply, is key. The UN's immunisation programme has been a success; the focus should now be on a vaccine against HIV.
**Hunger.** Use more land for food for consumption and less for cash crops.
**Trade.** The UN has urged all industrialised countries to abolish the barriers to free trade that punish exports from LEDCs. Fair trade ensures that people who produce the raw materials benefit more.
**Debt.** Governments of rich countries are slowly responding to pressure to write off foreign debt, but more needs to be done.
**Aid.** World governments at the 1992 Earth Summit in Rio agreed to work towards spending 0.7% of their GDP (wealth) on foreign aid. Only five countries meet that target. Britain spends 0.32%, the USA 0.1%.

**Key Words**
development • free trade

## ACTIVITIES

1. Write down two reasons why LEDCs are at a disadvantage when trading with MEDCs.
2. 'Aid to the South causes more problems than it solves.' Discuss this view.
3. Use the material on Worksheet 43 to discuss Fair Trade and working conditions in LEDCs.
4. In pairs, draw up a six-point Action Plan to 'Beat World Poverty'. Explain why you think each of the six policies you have chosen will be effective.
5. Log on to one of the following websites to investigate how aid agencies (a) collect donations, and (b) help people in poorer countries: www.christian-aid.org.uk, www.oxfam.org.uk.

# THE GLOBAL ENVIRONMENT

**There are many environmental problems that affect the global community. Sustainable development is one way to tackle these problems.**

## INTERNATIONAL ENVIRONMENTAL PROBLEMS

### USING UP RESOURCES

The Earth's natural resources are being exhausted through:

- Population growth. The world's population of six billion is estimated to grow to more than nine billion in 2050 before it stabilises.
- Development. Improvements in wealth and the standard of living lead to greater consumption of resources. The rich countries consume 80% of the total energy produced in the world.
- Action. Sustainable energy policies p.89.

### ACID RAIN

Acid rain is polluted rainfall, which affects countries in the northern hemisphere.

- Causes. Power stations, oil refineries and cars, which burn fossil fuels and give off waste gases (especially $SO_2$).
- Effects. Damage to trees, crops, water supplies and stone buildings. Acid rain may fall up to 2000 km away.
- Action. An EU directive demands drastic reduction in $SO_2$ emissions. This is possible through fitting filters in power station chimneys and catalytic converters in cars.

### DESERTIFICATION

Desertification is the spread of desert and desert-like conditions, at a rate of 12 million hectares per year.

- Causes. Drought, over-farming, deforestation, over-irrigation.
- Effects. Lack of vegetation, crop failure and famine in many LEDCs, especially North Africa.
- Action. Sustainable agriculture, planting trees, slowing deforestation.

### GLOBAL WARMING

Global warming is the rise in the Earth's average temperature.

- Causes. Burning too many fossil fuels, which release $CO_2$ and other greenhouse gases into the atmosphere, trapping solar energy. Deforestation also increases the amount of $CO_2$.
- Effects. Disruption in the world's climate, rising sea levels and flooding, spread of tropical diseases.
- Action. At the Kyoto Earth Summit in 1997 many governments agreed to cut $CO_2$ emissions. The UK has achieved its target, but the USA and other countries don't want to reduce their consumption of energy or their rate of growth.

### WATER SHORTAGE

In 1995, 40% of the world's population had no access to clean water.

- Causes. Population growth and consumption in the North; lack of water supply and sanitation networks in the South.
- Effects. Crop failure, disease and death.
- Action. Investment in water supply and sanitation networks; health education. The Johannesburg Earth Summit in 2002 agreed to work to halve the number of people without access to proper sanitation by 2015.

# SUSTAINABLE DEVELOPMENT

The extent of the global problems outlined on pp.84–87 is huge. Many of the world's governments met at the Earth Summit in Rio de Janeiro in 1992 to agree a way forward. They agreed on a policy of sustainable development, both for their own countries and for the world pp.90–91.

Sustainable development has four main objectives:

1. Economic growth, so that everyone can enjoy high living standards today and in future generations pp.54, 82–83
2. Social progress, so that the benefits of economic growth can be enjoyed in improved health, education, employment and the community pp.82–85
3. Careful use of natural resources
4. Conserving the environment.

## CONSERVING THE ENVIRONMENT

Conserving and protecting the environment is important to limit environmental threats, protect human health and safety, and protect wildlife and landscapes.

Environmental policies and pressure groups target several areas by:

- preventing pollution of air, land and water via waste dumping and dangerous chemicals
- cleaning up rivers, beaches and drinking water
- protecting wildlife habitats and the countryside and encouraging biodiversity
- encouraging sustainable agriculture through non-intensive farming methods which respect the environment
- encouraging sustainable forestry by planting trees to counter deforestation.

## USING NATURAL RESOURCES

Resources are either renewable or non-renewable:

- Renewable resources include water, wind, sun and trees. If they are used carefully they should last for ever, and they are less polluting.
- Non-renewable resources include coal, gas, minerals and oil. Once they have been used up they cannot be replaced.

**Sustainable energy policies aim to:**

1. make our use of energy more efficient, e.g. by reducing energy use at home and work, using cars less and public transport or cycling more
2. promote the use of renewable energy sources (alternative technology), e.g. wind, solar, wave, tidal and hydro-electric power.
3. save energy and preserve the environment by reducing waste and encouraging recycling.

## ACTIVITIES

1. **In pairs, look at the international environmental problems outlined on page 88. Discuss: (a) how we are all affected by them, and (b) how we are all responsible for them. Share your views in a class discussion.**
2. **'Sustainable development is development that meets the needs of the present as well as the future.' Explain in two sentences of your own words what you understand by this definition.**
3. **Log on to the Centre for Alternative Technology (www.cat.org.uk) and research two ways of using renewable energy sources. What advantages and disadvantages do they have?**

# WORKING FOR A SUSTAINABLE FUTURE

## LOCAL AGENDA 21

LOCAL AGENDA 21 UK

- One of the outcomes of the UN Earth Summit in Rio in 1992 was Agenda 21, an action programme for sustainable development signed by 179 countries, including the UK p.89➤.
- Two-thirds of the 2500 initiatives relate to local councils, following the principle 'Think globally, act locally'.
- Each local council has drawn up a Local Agenda 21 strategy to encourage their citizens to change their lifestyle so that it is more sustainable.
- Local Agenda 21 involves all sections of society, including schools, businesses, charities, community groups and individual members of the public.

# WHAT YOU CAN DO

## INDIVIDUALLY

Here are just some of the things you can do on your own to take responsibility for the Earth's problems:

1. Use the car less. Transport is the fastest-growing energy-consumption sector in the UK. It is also polluting. Instead, share car journeys, use public transport more, and make shorter journeys on bicycle or on foot.
2. Use energy efficiently. Individuals have little influence over how energy is produced, but we can control how we use that energy. Use insulation, energy-saving light bulbs and other eco-friendly products to conserve energy p.69➤.
3. Reduce consumption. Using too much energy and manufacturing (and buying) too many products put a strain on the natural world. Instead, use less heating, lighting and water to reduce fuel bills. Buy fair trade products for a fairer future p.69➤.
4. Recycle waste. Consumers in the UK produce about 16 million tonnes of domestic rubbish each year, most of which ends up in landfill sites. Recycling saves energy and raw materials as well as helping the environment and reducing pollution.
5. Eat well and exercise. Poor health does not help a sustainable society. A balanced diet and regular physical activity avoids many health and social problems.

## AS PART OF A GROUP

Here is information about just two of the many campaigns and pressure groups working for sustainable development in the community.

### FRIENDS OF THE EARTH

- Friends of the Earth is one of the leading environmental pressure groups in the UK.
- Over 90% of their income comes from individual donations.
- Its main strength is the 250 local groups, which campaign to improve the environment in their own area.
- It is also an international network of environmental groups working in 68 countries.
- Log on to www.foe.org.uk and click on 'Act local' to read some success stories and find out what your local group is doing.

### ECO SCHOOLS

- The Eco Schools programme encourages schools to adopt a sustainable lifestyle.
- The school draws up an environmental review, sets targets and plans campaigns.
- It takes about 18 months to implement the action plan before Eco School status is awarded.
- The programme involves the whole of the school community – parents, teachers, pupils and governors. (Log on to www.eco-schools.org.uk.)

# CHANGING SOCIETY

**Global problems can seem huge and insoluble. So what can ordinary people do to act as responsible citizens of the world?**

## HELPING THE LEDCs

### VOLUNTEERING ABROAD

- VSO is the world's biggest independent volunteer-sending organisation. It sends volunteers, not money, to help communities throughout the developing world.
- The volunteers are of all nationalities and come from every part of the community. They must have useful skills for instance, teachers, health workers, IT specialists, business people, etc.
- VSO prepares the volunteers for their placements and supports them while they are working in a developing country.
- A VSO youth programme is aimed at 17–25 year olds who want to be involved in international development work.
- Volunteering is also a fantastic opportunity to experience life and work as part of a community in a developing country. www.vso.org.uk

### HELPING FROM HOME

There are hundreds of charities, groups and campaigns that focus on solving the problems of LEDCs. All depend on volunteers for much of their work.

- Oxfam is one of the best-known charities in the world. It works for development and relief, finding solutions to poverty and suffering (www.oxfam.org.uk).
- CAAT (Campaign Against the Arms Trade) campaigns for the reduction and eventual abolition of the international arms trade, and of the UK's role in it as a leading arms exporter (www.caat.org.uk) p.81 ➤.
- Cafod (Catholic Agency for Overseas Development) is a Catholic charity which fights poverty in the South (www.cafod.org.uk).
- ITDG (Intermediate Technology Development Group) is an international development agency which specialises in helping rural communities in Africa, Asia and Latin America to develop and use sustainable skills and technologies (www.itdg.org).

**Key Words**

development • pressure group
sustainable development

## ACTIVITIES

1. **Look at the list of things you can do as an individual to promote sustainable development. How many do you do?**
2. **Use Worksheet 44 for a class discussion and then write a brief essay to explain the phrase 'Think globally, act locally'.**
3. **Local Agenda 21 encourages people to act in a way that will look after the planet. In groups, write an Agenda 21 for (a) school, or (b) home. Include proposals on transport, waste, water, energy, pollution and green purchasing.**
4. **Contact your local authority to find out what they are doing to implement Local Agenda 21. (www.scream.co.uk/la21 has a map to click on to with contact details.)**

# GLOSSARY

**Act of Parliament**
A law that has passed through the legislative process in Parliament, which ends with the monarch giving a bill royal assent. [Compare Bill]

**active citizenship**
The view of citizenship that stresses our participation in society, and which therefore focuses on our responsibilities as much as, if not more than, our rights.

**asylum seeker**
A refugee who applies for protection (asylum) in a foreign country for their own safety.

**bias**
Prejudice for or against a particular group, shown especially in the content or style of media reports.

**Bill**
A statute as it is proposed, before it becomes law as an Act of Parliament.

**budget**
A summary of expected income and expenditure for the next financial year.

**capitalism**
An economic and political system in which property and the means of production are in private ownership (rather than state-owned) and goods are produced for private profit. [See also free market economy]

**censorship**
A policy of examining publications, films, etc. in order to suppress anything considered politically unacceptable or obscene.

**citizenship**
What it means to be a citizen, including the rights, responsibilities and obligations that citizens have as members of their community.

**civil law**
The laws concerning the rights of individuals and their relationships with each other rather than the state. [Compare criminal law]

**common law**
The body of law based on custom, usage and the decisions of judges in specific cases (precedent). [Compare statute law]

**community sentence**
A sentence passed by a criminal court which requires the convicted person to do unpaid work in the community.

**constitution**
The basic rules or laws that set out the limits and powers of government and state the rights of citizens. Constitutions may be written or unwritten: the British constitution is partly written and partly custom.

**consumer**
A person who buys goods or services.

**contract**
A formal agreement between two or more parties.

**convention**
A formal international agreement, almost as binding as a treaty.

**criminal law**
The laws concerning the acts of individuals that are regarded as crimes against the state. [Compare civil law]

**crown court**
The type of court that deals with serious criminal cases.

**custodial sentence**
A prison sentence.

**decentralisation**
The reorganisation of government, or other power structures, to give greater power to the individual units (taking the power 'away from the centre'). [See also devolution]

**decolonisation**
The process by which colonies (countries ruled as part of an empire) gain independence from their imperial masters. Most British colonies gained their independence after the Second World War.

**democracy**
A system of government where the people, or their elected representatives, share power.

**deregulation**
The weakening or removal of rules and regulations to allow businesses to be more competitive.

**development**
Growth, particularly of an economic system.

**devolution**
The transfer of certain powers from a central government to regional governments. [See also decentralisation]

**direct democracy**
A system of government where the people take the decisions directly themselves. [Compare representative democracy]

**discrimination**
Treating individuals or social groups unfairly because of prejudiced views about those people based on their race, sex, religion, age, disability, etc.

**diversity**
Being different or varied; ethnic diversity means being composed of many different cultural or racial groups. [See also multicultural]

**electoral reform**
Reform of the system by which the members of a parliamentary body are elected. In Britain, supporters of electoral reform wish to replace a first-past-the-post system with a form of proportional representation.

**equal opportunities**
The idea that everyone should have the same rights and opportunities in life, especially in such areas as employment, education and housing.

**ethnic minority**
An ethnic or racial group that is distinct from the majority culture in a society.

**European integration**
Strengthening the institutions of the European Union to bind the individual governments more closely together into a unified whole.

**executive**
One of the three branches of government, concerned with making decisions and policies rather than with passing laws. In Britain the political executive is the prime minister and cabinet. [Compare legislature, judiciary]

**federalism**
A political structure or system of government (a federation) in which power is divided between a central government and other sub-units such as states, regions or provinces. [See also decentralisation]

**franchise**
The right to vote.

**free market economy**
An economic system in which the resources of a country are allocated through the free workings of the market (the 'laws of supply and demand'), with very limited government interference. [See also capitalism; compare planned economy]

**free trade**
The idea that countries should trade between each other without protecting their own economies from foreign competition by imposing tariffs, customs duties or import quotas.

**general election**
An election to choose the government of a country, in Britain held at least once every five years.

**globalisation**
The process by which the countries of the world are becoming more and more closely linked, through travel, trade, tourism and electronic communication.

**government**
The institutions that make the rules and decisions in a territory; also, the body which forms the political executive (as in 'the Labour government').

**House of Commons**
The main chamber of Parliament in the UK, also called the lower chamber, which debates government policy and passes legislation. It is made up of members of Parliament (MPs).

**House of Lords**
The second chamber of Parliament in the UK, also called the upper chamber, whose main purpose is to examine and revise laws. It is made up of unelected peers.

**human rights**
The fundamental moral, legal and political rights of the individual that are regarded as applying to everyone in the world.

**immigrant**
Someone who travels to another country in order to live there permanently.

**inflation**
A progressive increase in the level of prices for goods and services, brought about by an increase in costs or in demand.

**institutional racism**
The failure of an organisation to treat people fairly because of their ethnic origin or culture; it can be seen in attitudes and behaviour that are based on prejudices and amount to discrimination.

**interdependency**
When two or more people, institutions or countries depend on each other in certain respects, e.g. for trade or security.

**intergovernmentalism**
A form of cooperation between sovereign nation states. [Compare federalism]

**judge**
A public official who presides over all cases in the civil law courts, and over serious cases in the criminal law courts. Judges as a group are known as the judiciary.

**judiciary**
One of the three branches of government, concerned with interpreting and enforcing laws. The judiciary in Britain is made up of judges. [Compare executive, legislature]

**jury**
Twelve adults chosen at random who deliver a verdict in the crown court.

**LEDC**
A less economically developed country, from what used to be known as the third world (the 'South'). [Compare MEDC]

**legislature**
One of the three branches of government, concerned with passing laws. In Britain Parliament is the main legislative body. [Compare executive, judiciary]

**limited company**
A business that is owned by shareholders and run by a board of directors. A public limited company (plc) offers its share to the general public on the stock exchange.

**lobby system**
The briefings of confidential information given by the government to selected journalists in exchange for keeping quiet about their sources.

**magistrate**
The official in charge of a magistrates' court. Also known as a justice of the peace (JP).

**magistrates' court**
The court that hears all but the most serious criminal cases. Magistrates' courts are presided over by magistrates, or justices of the peace (JPs); there is no jury.

**mass media**
See media.

**MEDC**
A more economically developed country, from what used to be known as the first or second world (the 'North'). [Compare LEDC]

**media**
The means of communication that reaches large numbers of people, such as television, newspapers, etc. Also known as the mass media.

**mixed economy**
A mixture of the free market economy and the planned economy, in which resources are allocated by both the government and the private sector. [Compare free market economy, planned economy]

**multicultural**
Made up of many different ethnic groups or cultures. [See also diversity]

**nationalist**
Someone who believes that their country or national community should be independent, or have sovereignty over their own affairs.

**natural justice**
The principals of fairness and openness that determine how disputes are resolved between people or organisations.

**parental responsibility**
The responsibilities that parents have, such as to care for their children.

**Parliament**
The highest legislative institution of the UK, which consists of the House of Commons (the most powerful body), the House of Lords and the sovereign.

**partnership**
A business jointly owned and controlled by between 2 and 20 people; partnerships are common in the professions, such as lawyers and doctors.

**planned economy**
An economic system in which the state allocates resources, deciding who produces what and at what price; also known as command economy, and associated with the former communist countries of eastern Europe and the Soviet Union. [Compare free market economy]

**pluralism**
The idea that society consists of several different groups that share power or compete for power.

**political party**
An organisation of people with common interests who come together to pursue a political agenda and win elections to gain representation in the political system.

**prejudice**
An unfavourable opinion based on false beliefs rather than facts; also, intolerance or dislike of people of a particular race or religion, etc.

**pressure group**
A private, voluntary body that aims to influence government policy at local, national or international level without seeking election itself.

**private sector**
The part of a country's economy that consists of privately-owned businesses and enterprises. [Compare public sector]

**privatisation**
The transfer of public goods or services to the private sector. In Britain many industries owned by the state were privatised in the 1980s. [See also private sector]

**ublic sector**
The part of a country's economy that consists of state-owned institutions and services provided by local authorities. [Compare private sector]

**eferendum**
A ballot in which one issue is put to the electorate, and people decide by voting 'yes' or 'no'.

**efugee**
Someone who has fled to a foreign country because they fear persecution for their beliefs, religion, race or culture in their own country.

**epresentative democracy**
A system of government where one person acts on behalf of, or in the interests of, another. Elected representatives in the UK are members of Parliament. [Compare direct democracy]

**esponsibility**
A person or thing for which you are responsible; something you have control or authority over.

**ight**
Something that you are morally or legally allowed.

**ule of law**
The idea that human activity should be controlled within an agreed framework of rules or laws.

**eparation of powers**
The idea that the legislature, the judiciary and the executive should be separate from one another, to act as a check on government. Britain does not have full separation of powers because Parliament is both the supreme executive and legislative body.

**ingle currency**
The idea that all members of the European Union should have the same currency (the euro).

**ingle market**
A market consisting of a number of nations in which goods and money can move freely across borders without tariffs or other restrictions; one of the aims of the European Union.

**ole trader**
A business owned and run by one person, the proprietor, although s/he can employ others to help.

**overeignty**
The right to hold power and use that power. Parliamentary sovereignty means the power to make or repeal any law.

**spin doctor**
A party official or public relations consultant who tries to influence the way in which their party, policy or client appears in the media.

**stakeholder**
Someone who has an interest in a business or enterprise, as owner, employer, employee, customer, etc.

**statute law**
Laws made by a legislative assembly, such as Parliament in the UK. [Compare common law]

**stereotype**
A set of inaccurate generalisations about a group that allows others to treat them in a particular (generally unfair) way.

**subsidiarity**
The idea that the decisions of a political system should be taken at the closest possible level to the people affected by them. Applying to the European Union, subsidiarity means limiting the role of the EU to tasks that the states and regions themselves cannot carry out.

**subsidy**
A grant of money or other financial aid supplied to a particular industry, group or country.

**suffrage**
The right to vote.

**sustainable development**
Economic development that meets the needs of the present without adversely affecting the ability of future generations to meet their own needs. This means that economic growth must be accompanied by social progress, careful use of natural resources and conservation of the environment.

**trade union**
An association of workers in a particular trade or profession who join together to protect and promote their interests as a pressure group.

**transnational corporation (TNC)**
An organisation that operates in a wide range of companies across many countries, shifting economic activity around them to exploit local conditions. Also known as a multinational company.

**volunteer**
Someone who wishes to work for their community, or a foreign community, without being paid.

Published by Letts Educational
The Chiswick Centre
414 Chiswick High Road
London W4 5TF
Telephone: 0845 602 1937
Fax: 020 8472 8767
E-mail: mail@lettsed.co.uk
Website: www.Letts-SuccessZone.com

Letts Educational is a division of Granada Learning Limited, part of Granada plc



First published 2003, reprinted 2005

ISBN 184085 894X



**British Library Cataloguing in Publication Data**
A catalogue record for this book is available from the British Library.

**Acknowledgements**
The publishers would like to thank the following for permission to reproduce photographs and company logos (T = Top, B = Bottom, C = Centre, L= Left, R = Right):

Associated Press AP, p25R; Mary Evans Picture Library, p24B, p25T; Getty Images/Hulton Archive, p24T, p25CL; PA Photos, p27, p59, p81; Panos Pictures/David Dahmen, p53; Still Pictures/Mark Edwards, p79, Adrian Arbib/Christian Aid, p91C; Company Logos: ASA, p47TR, ITC logo supplied with permission of the Independent Television commission, p47TC, BSC, p47TCR, PCC, p47TL, VSO, p91T.

The author and publishers are grateful to the following for permission to reproduce copyright material.
This book was designed and produced for Letts Educational by Ken Vail Graphic Design, Cambridge

Commissioned by Helen Clark

Project management by Vicky Butt and Julia Swales

Editing by Nancy Candlin

Illustrations by Liz Bryan

Production by PDQ

Printed and bound in Great Britain